∨ ∨ ∨ ∨ ∨

ᐁ ᐁ ᐁ ᐁ ᐁ

Becoming and Remaining a People

Native American Religions on the Northern Plains

Howard L. Harrod

The University of Arizona Press   Tucson

The University of Arizona Press

Copyright © 1995

The Arizona Board of Regents

All rights reserved

♾This book is printed on acid-free, archival-quality paper.

Manufactured in the United States of America

06 05 04 03 02 01   7 6 5 4 3 2

Library of Congress Cataloging-in-Publication Data

Harrod, Howard L., 1932-

    Becoming and remaining a people : Native American religions on
    the Northern Plains / Howard L. Harrod.

      p.   cm.

    Includes bibliographical references and index.

    ISBN 0-8165-1583-2 (acid-free : cloth).

    ISBN 0-8165-1569-7 (acid-free : pbk.)

    1. Indians of North America — Great Plains — Religion. 2. Indians
of North America — Great Plains — Rites and ceremonies. 3. Indians of
North America — Great Plains — Social conditions. 4. Social change —
Great Plains. 5. Great Plains — Religious life and customs.
I. Title.

E78.G73H355 1995

306.6'99798 — dc20   95-32471

                                            CIP

British Cataloguing-in-Publication Data

A catalogue record for this book is available from the British Library.

In memory of my mother and father

Nettie Esther Smith Harrod
1898–1984

Howard Bailey Harrod
1887–1956

CONTENTS

Preface   ix

Acknowledgments   xiii

Introduction   xv

1   Social Change on the Northern Plains   3

2   Continuity and Change in Northern Plains Religions   19

3   Religious Development in the Village Societies   31

4   Religious Organizations and Ritual Processes   45

5   Religious Continuity and Change in the Village Societies   61

6   Religious Transformations on the Northern Plains   81

7   American Indian Religions and the Construction of Cultures   99

Notes   109

Bibliography   133

Index   141

PREFACE

The Great Plains has been host to many human populations in both historical and prehistoric times. The human cultures that emerged in the Plains environment before the rise of European dominance are the general focus of this study. Of particular interest are groups that occupied the Northern Plains, a vast and beautiful area that includes in Canada the southern parts of Alberta and Saskatchewan, and in the United States the present states of North and South Dakota, the territory in Montana east of the Rocky Mountains, the state of Wyoming, areas of northern Nebraska and western Minnesota, and the northwestern corner of Iowa.

The focus of this book is religion, an aspect of Northern Plains societies that cannot be clearly distinguished from other cultural dimensions. Religion is understood very broadly as a symbolic reality that is embodied in human experience through traditions and rituals. Religious symbols carried in oral and written narratives evoke in humans a sense of realms of meaning that are experienced as transcending the world of everyday life. Ritual processes sediment these meanings in experience and make them effective in thought and action. Understood in this way, religion casts a broad and complex web and gives rise to both the structure and the content of particular social worlds. The social forms of religion, embodied in shared traditions and enacted through rituals, also provide for the rise of individual religious experiences. In this interpretation, religion is as deeply personal as it is pervasively social.

The more specific concern of the book is to show how the oral traditions and ritual practices of Northern Plains religious systems developed and how they were transformed at critical points in time. Because religion is understood to be at the center of a process of human world-construction, an interpretation of the meaning of religious symbols and rituals leads to a partial disclosure of the complex social worlds that constituted the experience of the peoples of the Northern Plains.

On the Northern Plains, some of the oldest social worlds arose along the great Missouri River system, which provided both ecological and cultural possibilities for human development over a very long period. After the appearance of Europeans, the rivers gave traders, explorers, government officials, and missionaries access to the indigenous populations that had long resided there. Of particular interest is an area on the Missouri between the Knife and the Heart Rivers in the present state of North Dakota. As early as A.D. 1100, people with a distinctive culture and discernible religious forms were located in this region. They had migrated into the area, displacing or assimilating other groups who had previously lived there.

These people built earth lodge villages and developed a productive economy based on agriculture in the fertile river bottoms and hunting buffalo on the surrounding grasslands. In some of the earliest settlements there were spaces, sometimes near the center, that were probably places where religious activities occurred. Especially when these plazas were accompanied by an earth lodge larger than those surrounding it, the presumption of religious activity is even stronger. In the course of time, these lodge structures changed from a rectangular shape to the round shape that the first Europeans observed among the Mandans and Hidatsas when they made direct contact with them early in the eighteenth century. The village-plaza complex discloses very old religious motifs, which were expressions of symbolic systems and ritual processes that surrounded agriculture and hunting. In continuity with this older tradition, the Mandans and Hidatsas elaborated religious systems that related them in appropriate and productive ways to the plant and animal sources of their lives.

Understanding the religious symbols embedded in the oral traditions of

Northern Plains societies is essential for interpreting the relation of religion both to social identity and social change. These narratives sometimes became texts for rituals that shaped the social identity of groups, giving them a unique understanding of their origins. Ritual processes arising out of reinterpreted narrative structures also provided the means for reshaping the meaning of individual and social experience at critical points in time.

Another feature of Northern Plains cultural life had to do with the effect that human migrations had on basic religious forms and practices. These migrations, sometimes precipitated by the activities of European populations to the east, brought peoples into the region who developed social worlds and religious systems focused primarily on buffalo hunting. As a consequence of their entry into a new environment, some of these groups experienced significant social transformations and, in the end, became the typical Plains Indians that have populated the romantic imagination of generations of Europeans as well as North Americans.

Defined in this way, the problems illuminated in the course of this study are complex. On the one hand, I attempt to portray the development and changing character of rituals and systems of religious symbols among the village peoples. On the other hand, my concern is to understand how the development of new religious symbols and ritual processes enabled migrating peoples to make their transition to a new identity as nomadic buffalo hunters. In both instances, my intent is not to establish a core tradition from which Northern Plains peoples, whether village dwellers or nomadic hunters, have departed; rather, I am concerned with the way human beings interpreted and reconstituted their symbolic universes in the light of new circumstances. From this perspective, Native American rituals and symbolic systems were dynamic realities that changed through time. Some of these systems, such as those developed by the villagers, were more conservative and resistant to change, but none of the religions of Northern Plains peoples proceeded from a sacred canon or central body of literary materials. Their oral traditions were creative, changing realities that enabled them to reinterpret their experience as conditions surrounding them changed.

Trail Creek
Montana

ACKNOWLEDGMENTS

The support of a number of institutions has been essential to the completion of this work. The Rockefeller Foundation and the University Research Council of Vanderbilt University provided the resources that enabled me to spend an entire year on the preliminary research. The first part of this work was done at the University of Montana. The rich resources of the university library collection are always a pleasure to work with, and my friend Ray Hart smoothed the way for me when necessary. The D'Arcy McNickle Center for the History of the American Indian at the Newberry Library proved to be a fruitful place to do the second part of my research. The Newberry has a marvelous Indian collection and splendid work spaces. Of equal importance, the community of scholars gathered there at any given time provides a stimulating context for creative discussion and thought to occur. Special thanks go to Fred Hoxie and Jay Miller for their help and support.

I am grateful to Professors Douglas Knight and William R. Fowler of Vanderbilt University and Professor Kenneth M. Morrison of Arizona State University for their careful reading of the manuscript and for their comments. Two graduate students at Vanderbilt, Laura Frazier and Laurel Schneider, also read the manuscript, and I thank them for their thoughtful suggestions. Thanks also go to Michael Byrd, who checked the bibliographic references, and to Mark Justad, who prepared the index. My "outside reader" and friend, Donna Marx of Kalispell, Montana, made a number of helpful comments that improved the readability of the text and that I hope will make the book accessible to a wider audience.

Lucille Harrod Wasson and Jones Stanley Wasson of Holdenville, Oklahoma, are special family members who have also been parents to me through the years. I thank them for providing me with continuous support, affection, and the joys of kinship. Special thanks go to Annemarie who, in the midst of her own intellectual work and writing, has provided me with the companionship and friendship that are essential to this and all of my work. Finally, I would like to acknowledge my deep dependence on Northern Plains peoples, both past and present, whose religious traditions and practices are the subject of this study.

INTRODUCTION

This book is about the power that Native American religions have to preserve social continuity and to provoke social change, enabling groups to become and remain specific peoples. Its larger purpose is to bring into view the richness, depth, and cultural complexity of these past human beings and their contemporary successors. A significant problem with this and other similar studies lies in the sources on which interpretations are based. These sources include a wide variety of materials, ranging from the observations of early travelers, explorers, and fur traders to the writings of cultural anthropologists and archaeologists.

The members of the first group of observers were almost always severely limited by their cultural biases and economic interests, and the members of the second group were focused on theoretical concerns that emerged from their scholarly interests. In the case of both groups, then, there are interpretive difficulties: For the first group the problem is what we can discern about Native American societies after the cultural biases of these observers are critically assessed and set aside. A consequence of this process is that a number of interpretive gaps appear, and sometimes these gaps cannot be filled. For the second group the problem is to seek to reformulate their observations in the light of questions about the role that religion may have played in the production of social continuity and social change. Interpretive gaps appear in this material as well, some of which, again, cannot be filled. The problem in both cases is to discern the Native American voices in these materials and to bring those voices clearly to the surface. Putting the matter in this way suggests other questions.

Clearly, the observations of fur traders, explorers, and travelers during the eighteenth and nineteenth centuries are secondary in the sense that the Europeans and Americans, not the Indians, were the reporters of what they saw and heard, and many times the process of seeing and hearing was complicated by their inadequate knowledge of Indian languages and their cultural biases. But they were firsthand witnesses of many aspects of Indian life, and despite their problematic character, they are important sources for retrieving historical aspects of Native American religious traditions and ritual practices. While there is no assurance that Indian voices can always clearly be heard in such materials, the attempt is important because these observers produced the only written access we have to early cultural expressions of Indian societies.

The interpretive problems in the work of the second group, the cultural anthropologists, are complicated but somewhat different from those encountered in the reports of the fur traders, explorers, and travelers. Most of these individuals had engaged in a scholarly study of Indian languages, but not all were fluent in them. Some fur traders were more fluent because they lived for long periods within Indian communities, often establishing families with Indian women. Whereas the fur traders had clear economic interests in being associated with Indians, the cultural anthropologists were motivated to interpret them "scientifically" and to record their findings both for a particular scholarly community and for posterity. As a consequence of their work, museums were filled with artifacts dealing with many aspects of Indian life, skeletal remains of Indians were boxed for preservation, and institutions such as the Smithsonian, the American Museum of Natural History, and the Field Museum of Natural History sponsored massive documentary studies of material culture, social structure, language, and religion.

Studies of this sort are secondary in the sense that they produced interpretations of cultural realities, including religious traditions and rituals, that were constructed on the basis of theoretical perspectives that sometimes did not focus sufficiently on the internal meaning of religious systems and did not bring clearly into view the relation between religious meanings and social change or continuity. Nevertheless, what these anthropologists recorded, especially in the area of religious traditions and practices, was often descriptively very rich.[1] Some of these documents may be seen as primary in the sense that their authors were firsthand observers of ritual and narrative performances or because they were based on their informants' memories of past religious traditions and ritual practices. Oral traditions and rituals were reduced to writing, which removed them from the living level of performance, but there are significant continuities as well as discontinuities between traditions and rituals recorded in the early twentieth century and earlier observations made about these cultural realities.[2] In many instances, in fact, the Indian voices are much easier to hear than in some of the earlier observations.[3]

The fact that many later observations revealed continuity with a much longer past is an extremely important point. It makes clear, for example, that the anthropological record of oral traditions and ritual practices that researchers constructed on the basis of the memories of individuals is not as suspect as it might seem. Communities of memory in Northern Plains societies conserved tradition but also possessed the creative capacity to reinterpret traditions and practices. The work of the cultural anthropologists contains evidence of this dual process of conservation and innovation.

The fact that there was often a convergence between Northern Plains memories recorded in the early twentieth century and observations reported in the eighteenth and nineteenth centuries demonstrates that oral traditions and practices (or the memory of them) were being mediated, often in reinterpreted form, within Indian communities. The evidence for such an interpretive process is even stronger when we remember that very few Indians interviewed by cultural anthropologists in the early part of the twentieth century would have had knowledge of *written* sources produced earlier, but they had deep knowledge of their *oral traditions and practices*—and this is just the point. Knowledge and experience were organized into deeply shared structures of meaning upon which the creative imagination of the people worked, producing both the continuities and the discontinuities that were observed and recorded by the cultural anthropologists.

Given what has been said, this book is largely a text-based study that moves through several stages. Chapter 1 is concerned with reconstructing views of social change on the Northern Plains on the basis of what has been produced mainly by cultural anthropologists during the twentieth century. In this chapter I contend that these views are interesting and helpful but that they do not give sufficient attention to religion as a factor that both produces social change and maintains social continuity. On the basis of what is said in these studies, however, it is possible to reinterpret them, holding the role of religion at the center of attention. This process of reinterpretation begins in chapter 3.

Chapter 2 provides a broad synthetic overview of Northern Plains cultures that highlights religion as a source of continuity and change. In this chapter I show that the symbolic universes constituted by religious traditions and ritual processes became essential sources of social and individual identity. They also provided the people with access to power that was essential for the flourishing of individual and social life. For this reason, the symbolic boundaries established by religious traditions and maintained by religious practices were deeply resistant to change. Individual and social identity, once established, became sources of social continuity. In Northern Plains societies, social change also had important religious roots. Creative reinterpretation based on religious experiences, often in the form of dreams or visions, was one important element that shaped the responses of these societies to contact with other Indian societies and with European culture. Religious symbols also informed their interpretations of threatening events, such as the spread of epidemic diseases.

Chapter 3 reconstructs the long religious development of two village peoples, the Mandans and the Hidatsas. In this chapter I argue, on the basis of archaeological and ethnographic evidence, that these two peoples had a very long residence on the Missouri River. Their respective religious systems observed by early Europeans represented the result of a long process of social development and sedimentation. The Mandans, along with one Hidatsa group, had developed a sophisticated worldview, complex religious traditions and practices, and a very effective relationship with the surrounding ecosystem, its plants, animals, and landforms. Although two other Hidatsa groups were more recent migrants to the Missouri River than the first group of Hidatsas and the Mandans, they also had developed complex religious and cultural systems by the time they first met Europeans in the eighteenth century. Religious traditions and practices were essential sources of the social identities of these two peoples, and it was through their religious systems that they maintained their respective identities.

Chapter 4 elaborates in greater detail the major religious organizations and ritual processes that functioned to create and maintain the social identity of the Mandans and Hidatsas. Here I deal with religious enactments that were widely shared by the people. In addition to these ritual actions, which enabled them to relate to the plant and animal beings who provided them with food and access to transcendent powers, there were oral traditions that were sedimented in the experience of these peoples and that gave rich meaning to the ritual processes. In this chapter these oral traditions are woven together with the ritual processes that enact them.

Chapter 5 takes up the question of how the Mandans and Hidatsas—and by extension other groups on the Northern Plains—remained distinct peoples, often in the face of enormous social pressure. In this chapter I analyze the processes of creative reinterpretation that marked individual and social responses to greater interaction with Europeans, other Indian societies, and the new religion of Christianity. Processes of interpretation often linked newly appropriated elements of tradition to an older core and in this manner helped to maintain a sense of identity and continuity within the group. While to an observer the changes may sometimes have seemed radical, within the group a sense of continuity with an older tradition was often the more predominant social reality.

Nevertheless, there were examples of real religious transformations on the Northern Plains. Chapter 6 takes up two such cases: The Crows, who separated from the Hidatsas, developed their own special identity as a people; and the Cheyennes, who were migrants from east of the Missouri River, moved west of the river and became mobile, tipi-dwelling buffalo hunters. In this chapter I try to identify sources in religious tradition and ritual that are essential for understanding the social transformations that these two groups experienced. While the social processes involved in the movement toward their identities as nomadic hunting peoples were complex, I argue that religious traditions and practices were central to understanding how these developments took place.

Chapter 7 reflects more broadly on the relation between religious traditions and practices and the social construction of cultural identities on the Northern Plains. This chapter reiterates the thesis that religion was central to achieving a particular cultural identity as well as to initiating changes in it, and it concludes with some general comparisons with Euro-American society that arise when Northern Plains religions are considered from this perspective.

If there is a single broad understanding that holds these chapters together, it is that the religions of North American Indians are expressions of a general human capacity for religious experience, but each of these religions developed in a manner that gave the Indians' oral traditions and ritual practices a form and content that was distinct from other religions in the environment, whether Indian or European. Likewise, while the religions were affected by the appearance of Europeans and continue to be affected by the impact of Euro-American culture, Indians were not then and are not now passive spectators in the process. There was and is an Indian perspective at work producing both social continuity and social difference. Native American groups have often assimilated new religious elements either from Europeans or from other Indian groups, but they did not do so without actively reinterpreting traditions and rituals, reshaping them to fit their own needs. The development of any specific religious dimension among a particular people was grounded in the creative imagination of that people as it constructed, maintained, and reconstructed its cultural landscape.

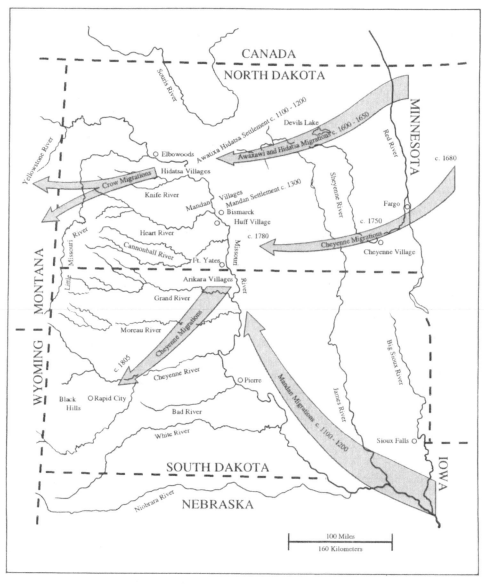

Missouri river village locations and population movements

▽ ▽ ▽ ▽ ▽

Becoming and Remaining a People

1 ⌄ ⌄ ⌄ ⌄ ⌄

Social Change on the Northern Plains

Native Americans have often interpreted their religious and cultural traditions as unchanging, seamless webs. From this perspective, these traditions had limitless horizons and were rooted in a deep, primal past. Native American peoples have seen themselves as ancient occupants of particular places, as having always been in a particular homeland. The special place of origin was sometimes interpreted as a gift from their creator, and was not simply a territory but the center of their world.

While such claims may be found among Native Americans of both the past and the present, understanding their meaning requires careful interpretation because extensive evidence shows that Native American traditions and societies were anything but static. Massive transformations deeply affected cultural traditions, and population movements brought groups into new territories. Long before the arrival of Europeans, the Northern Plains was the scene of both social transformations and resistance to change, of both alterations in self-understanding and the preservation of a sense of identity among particular peoples.

The attempt to understand social organization on the Northern Plains has a complex history. On the broadest level, interpreters have envisioned two different ways of life, two different cultural symbolizations.[1] One of these lifeways was developed along the Missouri River and its tributaries, and the river societies that followed it depended on extensive agriculture and periodic buffalo hunting for their subsistence. The people lived in earth lodge villages that at one time extended for at least five hundred miles along the Missouri in the present states of North and South Dakota. The other way of life was developed by Plains hunters who depended for their subsistence almost entirely on the buffalo, who lived in skin tipis, and whose rich cultures reached their climax in the middle of the nineteenth century.

When these two ways of life are compared, it is possible to see significant differences between them in political and economic organization, family structure, systems of social status, and religious symbolism. It is also possible to see some similarities. Thus the broad typology should not be interpreted so that the cultural expressions of the horticulturalists and the hunters are seen as mutually exclusive. The distinction should rather be thought of as a continuum with two poles and many shades of expression in between.[2] This is especially important because the horticultural societies had developed dual economies based on gardening and hunting, and some of the people who became nomadic continued to trade with the villagers for garden produce.

The question here concerns the way certain cultural forms and practices emerged among both village farmers and the hunting peoples, and how these forms and practices changed over time. At an even more concrete level, some social changes may have arisen as a consequence of interactions among earth lodge peoples themselves as well as interactions between earth lodge people and groups who were in the process of becoming Northern Plains hunters.

This way of stating the issues has an interesting history. Beginning early in this century, some interpreters claimed that the emergence of the buffalo hunting cultures could best be understood as a development of patterns that had their origin among the horticulturalists along the Missouri River, particularly the Mandans, who were among the oldest occupants. This interpretation rested mainly on the following evidence. First, a very old trading pattern among peoples on the Northern Plains brought village populations into contact with groups widely scattered over a very large area. The fur trade built upon this older network, and the coming of the horse stimulated increased contacts between buffalo hunters and villagers.[3] Second, there was evidence that many groups who later became horse nomads were themselves migrants into the Northern Plains. In 1800 there were at least eight groups on the Northern Plains: the three Algonquian-speaking divisions of the Blackfeet, with whom the Athapaskan-speaking Sarsis were allied; then there were the Atsinas, Crees, Assiniboines, and Crows. Prior to the beginning of the nineteenth century, all of these Northern Plains groups had been located elsewhere.[4] Some of the migrants had agricultural backgrounds, and some, such as the Cheyennes and the Crows, had an association with the earth lodge Indians in the course of their migrations. The Crows, for example, achieved their identity as Plains nomads after they separated from the Hidatsas.

The problem that the earlier interpreters tried to solve was how migrating peoples who possessed diverse backgrounds and cultures ended up in the nineteenth century as buffalo hunters with similar cultures. The idea that important aspects of Plains culture developed on the basis of patterns transmitted from the villagers was difficult to prove, for at least three reasons. First, oral traditions and social structures on the Northern Plains were notoriously hard to date, and thus their origins were often difficult or impossible to trace. Second, associating particular traditions or social structures with specific groups at precise points in time was a difficult and sometimes insoluble problem. Third, the identification of groups and the description of their movements were often hindered by ambiguity and large gaps in the evidence.

Despite these problems, it will be helpful to examine some of the explanations that were proposed for understanding social change on the Northern Plains. Early in the present century, Clark Wissler, an anthropologist who taught at Yale and who was also curator of the American Museum of Natural History in New York, made specific claims about the transmission of religious rituals and social forms.[5] Speaking of the Sun Dance, he said that "the Cheyenne or the Arapaho played the chief part in the distribution of the ceremony among the roving tribes."[6] He also argued that the Blackfeet "acquired the Sun Dance from the Gros Ventre [Atsinas], a division of the Arapaho."[7] While the Atsinas were culturally related to the Arapahoes, they were in close affiliation with the Blackfeet at the time of first contact.

Wissler was less certain that the age-graded societies that were so prominent among Plains groups had a central point from which they had spread.[8] His conclusion was that age-graded societies may have arisen among many different groups and that no one group may be credited with their origin. "The preceding discussion," he remarked, "is bringing us to the conclusion that no one group of people on the Plains can as yet be set down as the originators of Plains culture. There seems to have been a constant giving and taking until the whole area reached a general level of uniformity, bearing important differences . . . but differences that seem to be normal tribal variations rather than distinctive characteristics."[9] Wissler recognized that the complexity of the Plains situation made it difficult to locate a cultural center from which major institutions spread.

Despite these difficulties, Wissler attempted to identify social structures and patterns that would account for the way culture change seems to have occurred. For example, he showed that a fundamental condition that might foster change was the development of friendly relations among culturally diverse groups. These relations provided contexts for greater social interaction, and such interaction might stimulate processes of cultural interchange.

Guided by this hypothesis, Wissler grouped peoples on the Northern Plains according to the degree of their friendly relationship. He identified the Slave group, consisting of the Blackfeet, Sarsis, and Atsinas; the Siouan Algonquian group, consisting of divisions of the Assiniboines, the Plains Crees, and western groups of the Ojibways; the Algonquian Shoshone group, consisting of the Cheyennes, Arapahoes, Kiowas, and Comanches; and the Mandan group, consisting of the Mandans, Hidatsas, Crows, and perhaps the Flatheads.[10]

He also claimed that the Atsinas were go-betweens among Plains groups who were otherwise not friendly, and he argued that the Cheyennes traveled back and forth between the southern groups, such as the Tetons, and groups to the north on the Missouri, such as the Mandans. There were individuals within these societies who traveled extensively, who were competent in several languages, and who could reasonably be viewed as carriers of new cultural knowledge. "It was not unusual," Wissler said, "for an individual to wander away and reside for a time among other tribes, learning their languages and ceremonies."[11]

Wissler developed his notion of friendly relations out of his understanding of the ancient Plains practice of establishing kinship relations between groups that were otherwise not related by blood. The social processes that established such relations varied among groups, but a prominent example was the Peace Pipe, or Calumet, ceremony. In the Pawnee Hako ritual, for example, two hollow pipe stems, one understood as male and the other as female, were transported by an adopting group, the "fathers," to the group to be adopted, the "children." As a consequence of such adoption rituals, groups were bound together in ceremonial kinship relations that formed extensive networks on the Plains.[12]

Another cultural anthropologist, Robert Lowie, thought that village cultures were possible sources of social innovation on the Northern Plains. He demonstrated that there were similarities among the age societies of the Blackfeet, Atsinas, Arapahos, Mandans, and Hidatsas. What this fact must mean, he argued, was that "both the parental Arapaho and the Blackfoot must have been in intimate contact with the village tribes—the latter more intensely or in more recent times, . . . [but] since there is no documentary evidence for the historical connection of either the Blackfoot or the original Arapaho with the Mandan and Hidatsa, the proof of such contact, which alone renders the cultural facts presented intelligible, constitutes an historical conclusion of some importance."[13] Lowie believed that culture contact and interchange between hunting peoples and village Indians accounted for the evidence he presented concerning age societies. The problem was that he could identify neither material internal to tribal histories nor external historical observations to substantiate his interpretations.

Wissler also believed that such a connection accounted for the rise of many of the rituals on the Northern Plains. In 1915 he argued that the ritual similarities observed between the Blackfeet and the Pawnees justified the hypothesis that there must have been some cultural interchange between these two groups. Wissler claimed that the Pawnees were probably the originators of many of the ritual processes that were creatively appropriated by the Blackfeet, agreeing with Lowie that these cultural forms were probably mediated by the Hidatsas, Mandans, and Arikaras.[14]

The idea that the village horticulturalists were the source of much of what later became the culture of the buffalo hunters did not end with Lowie and Wissler. Almost forty years after their views were published, this interpretive tradition continued. Donald J. Lehmer argued that the material culture of the hunting peoples on the Northern Plains was probably based on the material aspects of the hunting dimensions of the earlier village cultures. On the basis of this claim he concluded: "it also seems likely that many of the more complex elements of the horse tribes' social organization [e.g., religion] were also transpositions from the older village pattern."[15] A few years later Edward M. Bruner repeated essentially the same argument when he said that "it is highly probable that the horse nomads adopted many aspects of the material culture, hunting techniques, social organization, and ceremonial practices from the well-established village tribes."[16] Finally, in 1970 Preston Holder argued that "if the horticultural complex and all of its structural ramifications were abstracted from the villages, there would remain the subsistence pattern and socio-political organization of the nomads."[17]

A complex example of cultural interchange between the village societies and the hunters that involved religious dimensions has been provided by Alice B. Kehoe.[18] She focused her analysis on the idea of transfers of power and on ritual practices in which power was mediated through sexual means. Sexual transfers of power were common among the village Indians, and Kehoe claimed that this practice seemed "to have diffused from the Mandan or Hidatsa to the three Algonkian-speaking northern Plains tribes with graded men's societies and to the Cheyenne, and to have acquired peculiar significance in the Algonkian tribes, which did not otherwise respect extra-marital intimacy."[19]

She also summarized Lowie's earlier evidence concerning the sexual transfers of power that appeared in age-graded society rituals. Graded societies were found, according to Lowie, among the Mandans, Hidatsas, Arapahoes, Atsinas, and Blackfeet. Age and purchase were the two conditions for entry into these societies. In addition, in some of these societies the purchaser surrendered his wife to an older man. In all five groups there was a comparable women's organization associated with the buffalo. In some of these groups implicit and explicit sexual meanings informed the relationship to buffaloes. On the basis of the fact that wife surrender was less well developed among the Algonquian groups than among the villagers, Lowie concluded that age-graded men's societies must have originated among the Mandans and Hidatsas and then been transmitted to the other groups.[20]

Kehoe argued that, among the Hidatsas, the sexual transmission of power was not associated simply with society membership changes but "was a method generally used by younger men wishing to obtain spiritual aid."[21] Among the Mandans, the custom was sometimes associated with symbolic intercourse with the buffalo, known as "Walking with the Buffalo." This ritual was an essential part of the Mandan Okipa ceremony, which was an important religious performance and which was believed by the people to be very old. Among the Hidatsas, sexual transfers of power were structured according to the father's clansmen. Since the Hidatsas were organized matrilineally, Kehoe believed that the ritual gave further weight to the father's clan as both the source of bundles, which were passed from father to son, and of ritual knowledge and spiritual power.[22] Such an arrangement, she argued, gave balance to a society that otherwise might have been completely determined by the matrilineal principle.

Among the Algonquians, sexual transmissions of power took on slightly different forms. Kehoe claimed that, among these groups, sexual transfers were more restrained by ritual boundaries than was the case for the Mandans and the Hidatsas. Even more restrained—indeed, interpreted as a ritual fostering self-restraint—was the Atsina case of membership purchase in the men's societies. Here the ceremonial "grandfather" was not supposed to have intercourse with the "grandson's" wife but rather was to pray over her as she lay exposed while he transferred a root from his mouth to hers without making sexual contact. This ritual was interpreted as a test of self-discipline for all parties: sexual discipline in the case of the grandfather and granddaughter, and resistance to the feeling of jealousy on the part of the grandson. The tensions were heightened by the practice of having the grandfather paint the naked bodies of the other two participants each morning of the ceremony.[23]

Among the Blackfeet, sexual transfers of power occurred only in the Horn society of the Bloods. In the transfer of membership, the ceremonial father touched his penis to the daughter's vulva. If he determined that she was chaste, he bent his forefinger into the shape of a buffalo's horn, bellowed like a buffalo bull, and had intercourse with the woman.[24] In the case of the Horn society ritual, unlike the rest of Blackfeet society, the virtue of chastity was acknowledged by inversion. Kehoe's conclusion concerning the Horn society practice was certainly not too strong: "a rather obvious fertility ritual used by the Mandan and Hidatsa to uphold the lineal structure of their villages was modified by the nomadic tribes to emphasize the value of self-discipline in the pursuit of tribal goals, among the strongly individualistic Blackfoot becoming perverted into an instrument of clique power."[25]

These explanations have located the sources of social change on the Northern Plains in various forms of interaction among the village societies and either nomadic hunters or societies that were in the process of becoming nomadic. Other explanations focused on broader factors, such as the fur trade and the acquisition of the horse.

In his analysis of the impact of the fur trade on Blackfeet culture, Oscar Lewis indicated that pottery was present among the Blackfeet in 1774, but that it seems to have disappeared from the cultural inventory of this society by 1800. According to Lewis, the reason for the disappearance of pottery was the establishment of trading posts in Blackfeet country after 1774 and the consequent increasing availability of iron pots.[26] The iron pots supplied by the traders displaced the traditional pottery that had been used by the Blackfeet. Significant changes in social structure also took place as the persons or groups who made pottery were themselves displaced. Often people who made pottery had a special social status that was sometimes associated with ritual practice. This status and its associated ritual practices were also undermined. Other items that disappeared as a consequence of the fur trade were the woven rabbit-skin robes that the Blackfeet acquired from the Flatheads, as well as the baskets that the Blackfeet used as serving dishes for buffalo meat.[27]

Lewis thought that social innovation among the Blackfeet was influenced by contact with the Mandans and Hidatsas. He argued that this cultural interchange happened after the 1820s and 1830s when the American Fur Company established posts that were visited by both the Blackfeet and the village peoples.[28] Even though direct and sustained contact may have occurred after 1820, the evidence presented earlier concerning the prehistoric trading patterns on the Plains suggest that the Blackfeet had indirect

contact with the villagers. The transmission of social knowledge and artifacts must have been going on for many years before the appearance of the
American Fur Company posts.

Lewis argued that developments in the system of Blackfeet age societies
occurred as a consequence of innovations introduced by the fur trade in the
early decades of the nineteenth century: "the increase in the number of age
societies took place at a relatively late period, probably in the eighteen thir-
ties or late twenties. This development would therefore coincide with the
period in which the expansion of polygyny and herding occurred."[29] He
concluded that the expansion of Blackfeet age societies helped channel the
vertical mobility that occurred as a consequence of an increase in wealth.
He further argued that the expansion of age societies among the Blackfeet
was the result of culture borrowing directly from the Mandans and Hidatsas
but that this cultural exchange simply expanded an age-grade system that
was already quite old.[30]

When he dealt with ceremonial bundles among the Blackfeet, Lewis
speculated that what he called the "bundle complex" may have appeared
sometime between 1787 and 1833.[31] It is interesting that in this early period women were not allowed to touch the pipes contained in the bundles,
while later transfer rituals included both the husband and the wife as the
essential social unit.[32]

The claims made by Lewis concerning cultural interchange between the
Blackfeet and the villagers have been given further support by the work of
John Ewers. Ewers identified a Blood Indian whom Prince Maximilian met
in 1833 as an individual known as Seen-From-Afar. Ewers claimed that this
Indian and his wife made visits to the Mandans and Hidatsas in the 1830s
and that these contacts were remembered by the elderly Bloods he interviewed. At least according to traditional Blood interpretations, "Seen-
From-Afar was credited with having brought back the Mandan pipe and its
ritual, a medicine bundle still owned by the Blood tribe. His wife brought
back a buffalo headdress of a Mandan or Hidatsa women's society and introduced it into the buffalo-calling ceremony of the Blood Indian women, the
Matoki."[33] If this tradition can be given credence, and there is no obvious
reason why it should not, then we have here a clear example of cultural
transmission involving religious elements.

At an even broader level, David Mandelbaum has analyzed the impact of the fur trade in Canada on the Plains Crees.[34] At the time of first contact, the Crees were depicted as an eastern Woodland group. Then between 1690 and 1740 the fur trade expanded into Cree country. Because the Crees were good trappers, used canoes, and knew the country well, they became major participants in the trade, supplying the fur trading posts. As a consequence of overtrapping, the game was depleted, causing some bands of the Crees to push farther west in their search for pelts. As they were now armed with guns, the Crees drove other groups, such as the Atsinas and Blackfeet, out of their territory.[35]

In addition to supplying pelts directly to the posts, the Crees engaged in trade with the Assiniboines and the village societies. Between 1740 and 1820 the Crees had expanded to their widest limits. The western bands had adapted their culture to a Plains way of life, while the eastern bands continued a Woodland culture pattern. Visiting among relatives and friends continued for a time between western and eastern bands, but by 1820 the bands in the west ceased for the most part to vacillate between the two lifeways. These people were ceasing to go to the woodlands and remained out on the Plains. The cultural transformations they experienced occurred as a consequence of their creative responses to new conditions introduced by the fur trade.[36]

Other studies deal with social change in a more sweeping manner.[37] George Hyde's analysis offers a sense of these approaches. His intention was to give an account of population movements that would illuminate the later history of some of the groups on the Northern Plains, and his thesis is worth quoting fully:

> [E]arly in the 17th Century the Red River country and the lands lying immediately west of Lake Winnipeg were held by Algonquian and Siouan tribes, most of whom were partly sedentary, dwelling in earth-lodges, making pottery, planting corn and some other crops. Among these peoples we may include the three Blackfoot tribes and the Atsinas, Arapahoes, Cheyennes, Hidatsas, Crows, Amahamis and, perhaps, the Mandans. After the middle of the century these tribes began to move, some toward the west and northwest, others toward the south and southwest. The evidence indicates that these movements were forced, and it strongly points to the Crees and Assiniboines as the in-

vaders who compelled the inhabitants of the Red River area to quit their old home.[38]

If these population movements took place in this manner, some of the associations among groups alluded to in oral traditions may have historical grounding. For example, according to some of these traditions, the Algonquian groups retained a memory that they were related at some time in the distant past. Old people among the Cheyennes considered their close relationship with the Arapahoes as a settled fact; they also thought they were related to the Crees and the Blackfeet.

In about 1825 a band of Blackfeet moved from Canada and settled among the Cheyennes living near the Black Hills in South Dakota. Most of these people married into Cheyenne bands and remained with them permanently; others joined the Arapahoes. Hyde argued that "It was apparently from talking with these Blackfeet that the older Cheyennes acquired the strong impression of their relationship to that people and their early association with them."[39] Some of the older Arapahoes thought their people had once been located northeast of the Plains, where they grew corn and lived a different life from the one they established as buffalo hunters. These Arapahoes thought that the Cheyennes and the Atsinas were kinspersons. In addition, the Atsinas and the Blackfeet were closely allied, and the Atsinas were connected with the Arapahoes.[40]

Hyde thought that the Cheyennes' memory of their previous life and location was clearer than was the case for other groups. "They had," he said, "a recollection of life in a cold land in the north where rabbits were hunted for food. . . . In that far-off time the people made seines and caught fish in the lakes. They traveled in canoes."[41] Cheyenne migration traditions showed that groups of people moved from their location northwest of Lake Superior, where they were living in about 1650, southward to the area of the upper Red River, where they met Siouan peoples who taught them to grow corn and live in earth lodges.

Hyde's description of the Cheyennes is of a people experiencing rapid social change, moving from an economy based on hunting small game and fishing in lakes to a predominantly horticultural existence that probably included as well the hunting of buffalo and smaller game. While the details are not known, the implication is that such changes affected not only the economic life of the people but also their polity, kinship system, and religious lives as well. Hyde extended his analysis of the Cheyennes to other groups: "if this happened to the Cheyennes when they reached Red River, is it not probable that it also happened to their kinsmen, the Arapahoes, Atsinas, and Blackfeet when they migrated into the same country?"[42]

Evidence in Arapaho traditions suggested that at one time the group lived northeast of the Missouri River, where they grew corn. Indians living in the nineteenth century had memories that during this period they used an ear of corn and a straight pipe in their religious rituals. By contrast, the Blackfeet situation was more difficult to trace since there was little traditional evidence to connect them with the Red River area, though there were clues in the historical record. In the eighteenth century, when the Blackfeet were migrating away from this area with the Atsinas, they possessed a bundle associated with elk and deer, suggesting an eastern origin, and as late as 1772 the Blackfeet made pottery and grew tobacco. On the basis of this evidence, along with that provided by other oral traditions, Hyde argued that "taking into account the known direction of the Blackfoot migration in the 18th Century this evidence indicates that the Blackfeet as well as the Atsinas and Arapahoes belonged to a group of tribes that in the 17th Century dwelt in the Red River country where they planted corn and other crops, made pottery and, perhaps, lived in earth-lodges."[43]

An interpretation that involves the horse and that paints an even broader picture of the sources of social change on the Plains was provided by Frank Secoy.[44] He argued that after 1600 there arose a vital culture that depended on the horse: "The adoption of the horse by the nomad hunters, in this case the eastern Apache, suddenly produced a highly active culture center on the Plains where none had existed before." Furthermore, "It was this culture center which developed that solid foundation of equipment, techniques, and activities upon which the late period erected the characteristic ceremonial, organizational, and decorative superstructure of the so-called 'Typical' Plains culture."[45] This culture center spread until by 1740 the Apaches, northern Shoshoneans, and Comanches occupied nearly half of the Plains area. Secoy's argument viewed religious innovation as part of a general process of cultural transformation, but he understood religion to be a part of the cultural superstructure that reflected more basic economic substructures.

In the third quarter of the eighteenth century, according to Secoy, another culture center arose that "approximated the region around the Black Hills and extended from there to the village tribes' sites on the Upper Missouri."[46] In this region, three important influences converged. The first was the impact of the Southwestern Plains center, which formed the basic pattern of nomadic Plains life; the second was the culture of the village groups; and the third was the pattern of the Northeastern Woodlands, carried mainly by people of Siouan descent. "The interaction of these three influences in this general area," Secoy argued, "fostered a phase of cultural creativity that was based upon the Southwestern Plains center, and that flowered into the superstructure of elements and complexes which distinguished Wissler's 'most characteristic' Plains tribes of the late 19th century."[47]

Following earlier interpreters, Secoy went on to hypothesize that both the form of the Sun Dance and the structure of the men's societies were developed during this period.[48] By the mid nineteenth century, this powerful culture center shifted west and south of the Black Hills and began to wane as "the flow of new cultural creations declined, and as the original developments were widely diffused and the original participating tribes, such as the Crow, Kiowa, Cheyenne, Arapaho, and the westernmost Dakota, were drawn off by migration to the west and south."[49]

An interesting comparative case involving the horse is Bernard Mishkin's analysis of the Coeur d'Alenes.[50] Before the arrival of the horse, these people were semisedentary, hunting, fishing, and digging roots along the rivers and lakes of their country. They used canoes and made baskets, but there is little evidence that they were settled in permanent villages. Changes introduced by the horse included increases in intergroup trade, contact, and intermarriage. In addition, larger amounts of meat and fish were transported along new or expanded trade routes. On the basis of this evidence, Mishkin argued that "Because of the widening of inter-tribal contacts the country inhabited by the Salish was completely opened to influences from the east and Plains traits were rapidly diffused through the region. Tribes such as the Thompson and Shuswap which were hardly exposed to influences from the Plains and Southeast, before the horse, received many Plains traits."[51]

To fill out this picture, James Teit's description of the impact of the horse on Coeur d'Alene culture deserves to be quoted in full. The horse, he said,

> drew them away from the lakes, and in great measure from fishing, canoes, bark, and wood, materials which they were accustomed to use. They could not follow the old life on the water and in the forests, and at the same time keep horses. Besides, as raising and herding horses and buffalo hunting necessitated much travel, the people had no time for their former industries. Furthermore, many of their utensils were unsuitable for the new style of life. Objects made of wood, bark, and basketry were either too bulky, cumbersome, or fragile; therefore they were largely dispensed with. Bags of skin, leather, and rawhide took the place of basketry and woven bags because they were better suited for travel by horse. Instead of the former small hunting parties, consisting of people of one band or part of a band, hunting now became largely a tribal business, and demanded a different organization. The easier method of making a living offered by buffalo hunting, as well as the pleasure and excitement of traveling and mingling with strangers, which it afforded, were great inducements. Once horses were plentiful, intercourse became easy and general between all members of the tribe, and buffalo hunting as a tribal affair could be engaged in. The old system of chiefs of bands and divisions became obsolete, and only tribal chiefs continued to be recognized. There were really no more bands or divisions. The change from a tribe consisting of many semi-sedentary bands with as many headquarters to a single, almost entirely nomadic community, with a single center, was in time almost completed. The old communal dance houses were abandoned and dancing was conducted entirely in camp circles.[52]

Teit's close description of social changes involved in the movement toward Plains culture patterns showed how innovations occurred at many important levels of social life, including religious practices.

In addition to the factors discussed above, more recent interpretations give weight to the impact of the epidemic diseases that accompanied the fur trade, as well as earlier culture contacts.[53] Certainly this harsh reality must be taken into account, for it clearly explains—as warfare, the horse, the gun, and the economic aspects of the fur trade by themselves do not—why so many Native American groups had to reorganize their societies. As a consequence of amalgamation forced by the decimation of their populations, many groups apparently did engage in creative social innovation.

All of the interpretations reviewed in this chapter focus on social changes that deeply affected and sometimes radically reshaped the lives of American Indian peoples. Explicitly or implicitly, each of these treatments deals with changes in religious institutions and ritual processes. Sometimes missing in these views, and not clearly expressed in others, is a more detailed sense of how religious transformations actually took place and what some of the central explanatory factors may have been. Especially muted in these explanations are discussions of the impact of Indian intentionality, interpretation, and agency on the nature and character of change. The next chapter provides a perspective that brings into bolder relief the importance of religious symbols and ritual processes for explaining both social change and social continuity in Northern Plains societies.

2 ⌄ ⌄ ⌄ ⌄ ⌄

Continuity and Change
in Northern Plains Religions

The interpretations of social change reviewed in the last chapter need to be expanded in the light of a perspective that focuses on the role that religion played in the constitution of individual and social identity, as well as in the production of social change, in Northern Plains societies. This chapter provides a context for interpreting the experiences of particular Northern Plains peoples. The remaining chapters use this perspective to interpret specific instances in which religion was crucial for understanding how social continuity was maintained and how social change occurred. At the center of this view is the argument that it was through religious experiences that individuals on the Northern Plains came to a sense of personal identity and that religious practices provided essential aid to persons in each of their life stages. Furthermore, it was through the symbolic boundaries established by religious traditions that particular groups distinguished themselves from other societies in their environment, and it was through shared religious practices that this sense of separate identity was maintained and periodically renewed.[1]

The energies released in religious experiences and practices not only provided a sense of identity and continuity but also enabled individuals and societies to respond creatively to the emergence of novelty in their environment. Whether novelty was imposed as a direct or indirect consequence of the European presence, pressures from other Plains societies, or conflicts internal to the group, religion played an essential role in determining the direction and shape of social change. If individual and social identity was threatened, religious experiences and practices were central to any successful social reconstruction. If the threat was traumatic, such as the spread of epidemic disease, religious energies sometimes played a creative role in projecting a new or drastically reorganized social identity.

A sense of social continuity and identity was evoked in the experience of Northern Plains peoples through their participation in the religious meanings embodied in powerful reservoirs of shared memory. This shared memory was richly textured and included explanations of how the land, which dominated everyday experience, took shape; interpretations of how humans, animals, and other powerful beings came into existence; and narratives about how the special identity of the people was formed.

Origin traditions provided an account of the rise of the landforms occupied by various Northern Plains peoples. According to these traditions, particular landscapes arose as a consequence of the exploits of one or more creator figures. In these traditions, creator figures were often not clearly distinguished from another ubiquitous presence: the trickster. Sometimes appearing as Coyote or another animal, trickster figures were often involved in the creation or transformation of the world. In some traditions they exercised their powers alone, while in others they worked in cooperation with or in tension with the creator or creators. Tricksters in these traditions exuded a gross physicality. Their appetites were seldom if ever under control. They roamed the world seeking an easy meal, engaging in sexual trickery and exploitation, or suffering the consequences of their own foolishness. They often violated the accepted moral order of the groups in which they appeared. Perhaps for this reason their exploits were sometimes used to socialize children in appropriate forms of behavior. Despite their morally ambiguous qualities, trickster narratives were extremely widespread and popular among Northern Plains societies.

In many origin traditions, creator figures were assisted by diving birds or animals who brought earth from below primal waters. Out of this earth the land was formed, sometimes taking shape in relation to the four cardinal directions. The creator figure also shaped the more specific features of a people's environment. In Mandan and Hidatsa societies, for example, the environment was dominated by the Missouri River and its tributaries, as well as by more concrete landmarks such as the buttes and breaks along the streams and rivers. In addition there were animals such as the buffalo, bear, deer, and elk; and there were plants such as beans, corn, squash, and sunflowers. An extremely important plant, which was central to religious practice, was tobacco.

These animals and plants were not only food sources; they also appeared to the people in their visions and dreams. In the world of everyday experience, they existed as concrete plants and animals, but in their dream forms they transcended the world of everyday life. When they appeared in the dream or vision world, it was usually in the form of persons who possessed extraordinary powers that were essential for the people's lives, and when they were encountered as the animals and plants of the everyday world, they were believed to possess consciousness and purpose, and they formed their own societies to which the human world was related.

The formation of the human body often proceeded by means of a series of experiments or mistakes by the creator, which included the creation of males and females in the human world and sometimes the animal world as well. In some traditions, humans were formed in the hollow of trees or made out of mud or other materials. Animals and plants, as well as humans, were sometimes represented as beginning their existence underground and emerging into the world above at a particular time. There were many variations on these traditions, but in most of them there were some animals that were not created but instead were present with the creator and assisted in the formation of the world.

In many traditions, the foundation of the experienced world included as well an explanation of the order of life, death, and gender relations. Humans were represented as flourishing in the land, having been provided by the creator with an abundance of plant and animal food. Animal skins were available for clothing, and lodges could be constructed either out of these materials or from the earth and wood that were readily available in the stream and river bottoms. Life was rich, but suffering also came to humans, and death was the final outcome. Northern Plains traditions accounted for death in many ways. In some instances, death became the fate of humans as the result of a wager between creator figures. Sometimes the dead remained in communication with the living. In many traditions the ancestors were believed to travel to a land of the dead, where they lived on, following an existence that was much the same as their earthly lives. In some traditions, particular features of the land of the dead were portrayed as opposite to the world of the living. In the land of the dead, for example, ancestors might hunt at night and sleep during the day.

The primordial order of gender relations was sometimes alluded to in these traditions. In some instances, males and females were portrayed as initially living apart. Then, through some means they were brought together, marriage arose, and children were born. Some more specific traditions described a normative division of labor between males and females, although many traditions were incomplete or unclear on this point. Often gender relations were more specifically shaped by traditions and ritual practices that surrounded two main economic activities: hunting and agriculture. In many instances there were people who formed a third gender in Northern Plains societies. If they were male, they fulfilled many of the roles that were usually assigned to females, such as gardening or bead work. If they were females, they might hunt, go to war, or perform other roles that were usually assigned to males. Sometimes these third-gender roles involved sexual relations—gay and lesbian behavior—but in other instances sexual expression seemed to be lacking. In either case, these individuals often played important religious roles in the societies.

In some Northern Plains origin traditions, people were portrayed as arising at particular places, such as the mouths of the Heart or Knife Rivers where they flowed into the Missouri. The people were created in this place and no other. This place was evocative and over time became an essential feature of the people's self-understanding. Some Mandans and Hidatsas, for example, so understood themselves. The places of residence of these historical peoples were therefore perceived and understood through a network of religious meanings.

Origin traditions may be distinguished, though not separated, from narratives concerning the relation of Northern Plains peoples with other special and powerful persons who appeared in both male and female form. Sometimes these culture heroes were not clearly distinguished from creator figures. In many traditions they led the people in migrations to their historical homelands, and in most they were responsible for bringing important gifts of power to the people when they were experiencing times of great stress.

In some instances, migration narratives began with the theme of emergence from below a lake or other underground source. In other instances, migrations began from a place that was represented, often vaguely, as being far from the people's present homeland. The description of these long-ago places included images of a life that was very different from the one that the people presently enjoyed. The narratives sometimes revealed fragmentary images of major social changes that the people underwent during the course of their migrations. The traditions were passed on, sometimes in reinterpreted or expanded form, to succeeding generations. There was little doubt in the minds of those who shared them that the mountains, rivers, animals, plants, and other persons, human and nonhuman, would continue to exist; and they were certain that the life-giving rain, the flowing waters, and the winds from the four directions would nourish the lives of their children as they had their own. They were people of *this* land and place; this was and would remain their special identity and destiny.

Along with religious traditions, religious practices were also central to the people's lives. These practices enabled individuals and societies to act appropriately toward the plant, animal, and other life forms in their environment. Appropriate action resulted in an abundant harvest or a successful hunt, providing nourishment essential for life. Religious practices were also important for insuring good health, for overcoming the powers that caused illness, and for healing the wounds that were common occurrences in everyday life and in war. Religious practices were required to neutralize enemies or overcome their power in the event of conflict.

In all of these contexts, religious practices on the Northern Plains usually took the form of ritual processes that released the power residing in religious objects known as bundles. Bundles were believed to have originated in the vision experiences of a contemporary individual or a predecessor, or as the result of a gift from a culture hero. Bundles were composed of a variety of things: pipes, earth paints, plant materials such as sweetgrass to be used as incense, animal skins, stones, animal bones, and other materials. These items were wrapped in one or more animal skins and were secured by leather thongs.

In a profound sense, Northern Plains peoples believed that bundles were alive and that their power could be released into the world through effective ritual action. This belief was based on the view that nonhuman persons such as Otter, Buffalo, Elk, or Corn had given their special powers to an individual in a vision or had mediated these powers through a culture hero. These powerful others had specified what was to be in particular bundles, how they were to be cared for, and how their rituals were to be enacted. If the ritual action was done correctly, a hunt would be successful, a wound would be healed, an enemy would be overcome, or rain would fall on a thirsty garden.

Some bundles were associated with the well-being of groups or even the entire society, and others were related to the needs of particular individuals. Since the needs of the individual were not clearly distinguished from those of society, the functions of these two classes of bundles often overlapped. Smaller bundles that assisted hunters or protected individuals during battle were common. Some of the larger bundles that related to the needs of the group performed these functions as well.

Bundles that held power for hunting and for gardening, and the rituals that enacted their power, expressed in a concrete manner the relationship between the genders in Northern Plains societies. Hunting bundles were often given to men by male culture heroes or male animal persons, although there were exceptions to this rule. Agricultural bundles were associated in some societies with female culture heroes, although again there were important exceptions. Ritual knowledge surrounding these important life activities drew a symbolic boundary between the genders and created a division of labor between them.

Because bundles were associated with important cultural values, they tended to be resistant to change, and because they were given by nonhuman persons to individuals who were members of particular groups, their origin traditions and rituals tended to become a deep part of the self-understanding of these people. Along with religious traditions that embodied the actions of creator figures, bundles and their ritual processes became formative for the Northern Plains world experience. In many instances, the religious traditions, along with their nonhuman figures, became dramatized in the rituals of specific societies.

Bundles were connected not only to important activities in the life of an individual but also to other more complex rituals that released energies believed to be efficacious for the society as well. The various sun dances on the Northern Plains often had one or more bundles at the core of their ritual processes, and both the Mandan Okipa (a ritual of great complexity) and the Sacred Arrow ceremony of the Cheyennes were focused around bundles that were essential to the people's life as well as their success. These more elaborate societal rituals often dramatized the migration traditions of the group, their creator and culture hero stories, and their special homelands. In this manner, the symbolic forms enacted in these rituals deepened and sustained the identity of the people.

Religious traditions and practices nourished a sense of continuity in the experience of Northern Plains peoples, not only because they became routinized and finally stable and accepted aspects of their social worlds but also because they confirmed the legitimacy of certain divisions of labor and justified the way social power was structured. These factors also contributed to the maintenance of symbolic boundaries between groups.

Bundles were in the possession or under the care of ritually and religiously qualified individuals who were bound by the rules that surrounded these living entities and who also served as custodians of the knowledge of ritual processes by means of which the bundle's power was released. Social power in Northern Plains societies was acquired through religious experiences and through the ownership or control of religious powers released through bundles. Persons who were ritually and religiously qualified occupied a higher status and exercised more social power than those who were recipients of the religious energies released through bundles when they were enacted in rituals. These ritually and religiously qualified persons were often elevated to positions of political leadership; they gained wealth as a result of gifts that were given as payment for exercising their ritual knowledge in bundle openings; and they were often prominent leaders in major religious ceremonies.

Because of the close relationship between religious experiences, religious practices, and social power, resistance to change and a desire to preserve religious continuity were common in Northern Plains societies. Whether a bundle was owned or only kept by a qualified individual, elaborate rules in most of these societies governed the transfer of a bundle and its power. Generally, the transfer was structured either by kinship or by an exchange of property between two unrelated individuals.

If the control of major bundles was based in kinship patterns, bundles might be inherited, following either the father's or the mother's line, depending on the societal pattern. No matter what the pattern of descent, the ritual knowledge associated with the release of the bundle's power was carefully guarded and was passed systematically to the appropriate kinsperson or family group. In this system, both the individual owner or keeper and the family group also received the social status and power associated with the bundle and sought to keep them intact. If bundles were transferred from one unrelated individual to another, the extended families still participated in gathering the wealth necessary for the exchange and gained the social influence that went with bundle ownership. In this case as well there was an attempt to control access to social influence and to transfer the bundle to those who were qualified by virtue of their religious experiences and their social status.

Dreams and visions, as well as induced suffering and physical deprivations, shaped the primary content of religious experiences among Northern Plains peoples. Since there was such a close relationship between religious experience and social status, the quest for visions and dreams, and for honorable occasions upon which to endure suffering, were prominent features of these societies. The life chances for young men—and in some groups for young women—were vastly enhanced by a successful vision quest, although the quest for power did not necessarily end with youth but often continued throughout an individual's life. The sun dances and other ritual processes provided occasions for individuals to endure the suffering that was requisite for religious experience. In some Northern Plains societies, powerful dreams or visions, combined with appropriate suffering, might qualify individuals to become bundle owners. For this reason, social controls governed such experiences. Older individuals who were religiously or ritually qualified and who were or had been bundle owners became gatekeepers, who interpreted the meaning of dreams or visions to younger persons. Control over the interpretation of dream and vision experiences provided some limitations both on which and how many persons could share in bundle ownership and on the social privileges that followed from such ownership. This conservative factor was another element contributing to resistance to social change within Northern Plains societies.

Kinship groups or individuals who formerly owned bundles did not lose all of the advantages of their social position after a transfer ritual occurred. Former bundle owners were held in high esteem, and family groups in which bundles had resided were looked upon as higher in social status than those families that had been less fortunate. Individuals who had formerly been directly related to bundles were often allowed to participate in their rituals or were elevated to positions of religious or political leadership.

No matter what the patterns of ownership and transfer were, the power of major bundles circulated throughout most Northern Plains societies. This power, focused as it was around core values having to do with essential life activities, was believed to be ultimately of benefit to all and for this reason could not be dominated by any one individual or group. Even though there were occasional examples of individual or group aggrandizement, social pressures existed that militated against such egoistic tendencies.

Social continuity within Northern Plains societies was constituted by shared worldviews and common religious practices that were specific to each group. These worldviews arose out of cultural symbols that embodied the activities of powerful others who transcended, yet at the same time gave rise to, the world of everyday experience. Images of origin and destiny supported the sense of identity among peoples and maintained cultural boundaries between groups. If social continuity was constituted and maintained by such powerful symbols, how are social changes to be understood, and what is the role of religion in social change? The previous chapter showed that many early interpreters located the sources of social change in consequences that flowed from the impact of European contact. European contact brought not only new cultural items, such as iron pots, guns, and horses, but also epidemic diseases and powerful but alien cultural values.

While these interpretations are not to be dismissed, what is needed now is a view that emphasizes the importance of religion for understanding the responses of Northern Plains societies to novelty in their environments.

In addition, we need to understand how a sense of continuity was maintained in the experience of people who were undergoing social change. The essential point is that cultural interchanges, whether between Europeans and Northern Plains societies or among Northern Plains societies themselves, did not always lead to an *experience* of fundamental social change. A sense of continuity was maintained in the experience of many groups because their cultural identities, grounded in traditions of origin and evoked in ritual processes, were reinterpreted. The process of reinterpretation often preserved a sense that the world experience and the basic identity of the group were intact. How this happened requires further explanation.

When novelty, threat, or perceived danger appeared in Northern Plains social worlds, traditional methods of interpretation came into play. Seeking visions was the socially accepted method for dealing with both internal and external threats. In such circumstances, religiously qualified people, such as bundle owners or keepers, sought counsel in their dreams and visions. The results of these experiences motivated interpretations of the meaning of novelty and also suggested modes of response that were viewed as being in continuity with the self-understanding of the society. From this perspective, social change needs to be interpreted in relation to the creative responses of human agents as they struggled to reconstitute their worlds.

Because dreams were so pervasive in these societies, individuals who were at the margins of the group and who were lacking in social power might make their own contributions as well. There were many narratives in the oral traditions, for example, that told of powerful dreams and visions that arose in the experience of socially marginalized, sometimes anonymous, individuals. Sometimes they became important sources of social innovation. But for the majority of dream experiences, the successful legitimation of new interpretations required the cooperation of past and present bundle owners. If such legitimation occurred, the reservoirs of memory that mediated a sense of continuity in social life and that maintained the symbolic boundaries that constituted the identity of the group were reshaped.

Given these complexities, social change needs to be interpreted from at least two perspectives. On the one hand, interpreters of the Northern Plains cultures rightly focused on traumatic or externally induced social change as a characteristic and pervasive feature of these societies. On the other hand, looked at from within these societies, many Northern Plains peoples experienced continuity more predominantly than change. Reinterpretation sometimes led to an expansion of tradition rather than to a sense of rupture and social crisis. It is essential to understand these societies from both of these perspectives.

There were times when Northern Plains societies experienced a social transformation that led them to form a new identity. In these cases, the patterns of religious leadership, religious experience, and social legitima-tion that have been discussed were employed as groups moved toward a new social identity. The outcome, however, may not have been the ex-pansion of shared traditions but rather the construction of new traditions that became, over time, socially routinized and taken for granted. For ex-ample, among people moving from semisedentary agricultural economy to a predominantly nomadic hunting economy, the emergence of a new self-understanding sometimes depended on the appropriation of different or re-interpreted origin and culture hero traditions. The culture hero may be interpreted as leading the people to a new homeland, bringing them the gift of bundles focused on hunting rather than agriculture. New societal rituals may also be introduced at this time. Reinterpretation that led to social transformation often depended for its motive power on religious in-novations. It is this element that is not fully elaborated in the interpreta-tions described in the previous chapter.

This perspective on the relationship among religion, social continuity, and social change must be interpreted in a manner that preserves the com-plexity of the Northern Plains situation. The creation and maintenance of a people's identity over time does not refer to a state of social stasis. Neither should this perspective be mistaken for a version of the claim that Native American cultures were primal, unchanged in their essence once they were constituted. Rather, the groups who lived on the Northern Plains became identifiable peoples through creatively constructing shared social meanings that led to the emergence of specific societies. These societies did not con-struct their social identities out of nothing. Even the older occupants of the area, such as the Mandans, had a history and came from other places, experiencing social change and perhaps significant transformations in the course of their migrations. The construction and maintenance of their identity as a people were historically emergent, and the sense of continuity that they possessed had more the quality of a moving equilibrium than of stasis or the realization of an unchanging social essence.

These perspectives on the role of religion as both a stimulus for social change and a factor in the maintenance of social continuity need to be applied to more concrete historical materials. To do this, the rich and complex histories of the Mandans, Hidatsas, Crows, and Cheyennes are analyzed in the following chapters. The Mandans and some of the Hidatsas who lived on the Missouri River had long ago migrated to their homelands and possessed well-established social organization. They had become a people, and they remained a people during the initial phases of European contact. In a fundamental though not unchanging sense, they remain a people today. In the course of their migrations, some Cheyennes became earth lodge people for a time before they moved on to become mobile buffalo hunters, and the Crows became a separate people only after their split with the Hidatsas. Religion was an essential ingredient in the creation and maintenance of the social identities of all these peoples, and religious energies were foundational in the construction of new social identities as they responded to either imposed or chosen alterations in their environment. In the light of this perspective, the next chapter begins a process of reinterpretation of ethnographic material gathered by cultural anthropologists and others.

3 ⌄ ⌄ ⌄ ⌄ ⌄

Religious Development
in the Village Societies

The understanding of religion elaborated in the last chapter becomes convincing only if it illuminates actual cases of continuity and change on the Northern Plains. In order to test the interpretive power of this perspective, we will retrieve and reconstruct the traditions and ritual processes that formed the religious universes of two village societies, the Mandans and the Hidatsas, focusing particularly on the way their worlds were formed, how they were maintained, and how they were changed. The cultures of the peoples who occupied the Missouri River and its tributary system had developed over a long period and were quite complex by the time of European contact in the middle of the eighteenth century. To provide a broader context for interpretation, we need to gain a sense of the history of settlement along the Missouri River before turning to an analysis of religious traditions that were essential for the emergence of the Mandans and Hidatsas as peoples.[1]

The peoples who lived in the Missouri River region of the Northern Plains before the emergence of the Mandans left evidence of buffalo hunting and agricultural activity. Archaeological sites that exhibited such features were found in the eastern Dakotas and along the Missouri River in western North Dakota. While buffalo hunting was essential to the economic lives of these earlier Missouri River populations, it is also important to grasp the ritual significance of this animal. For example, the Boundary Mound burial site is located on the Missouri River on the border between North and South Dakota. Buffalo skulls were placed around the burial pit before a mound was erected over the top. These skulls had the remains of red earth paint on them, indicating that they probably had religious significance. Such burial mounds were typical cultural features in the region, and the presence of buffalo skulls was widespread. In addition, these people made conoidal pottery vessels and hunted with the atlatl and almost certainly with the bow and arrow.

Beginning about the eighth century, groups of semisedentary agriculturalists began moving into the Missouri River valley, occupying most of southeastern South Dakota. These people built their villages on high terraces above the floodplain of the river, often near the mouth of a large tributary stream. The occupation of these villages spanned the period from about A.D. 700 to 1200, and they were characterized by "long-rectangular houses often fortified by dry moats and palisades, with people relying on horticulture but with heavy emphasis on the hunting of bison, deer, and lesser game."[2] In addition, they depended on fishing to some extent, as did the Mandans and Hidatsas later.

The earliest village sites that may represent a cultural stream similar to the later Mandan and Hidatsa groups appeared between 1100 and 1400. The villages were small, containing between fourteen and forty-five rectangular houses, and they normally occupied from four to seventeen acres of land. The more than one hundred sites that can be identified with this population were distributed along a five-hundred-mile stretch of the Missouri River between the Little Missouri River in North Dakota and the White River in South Dakota. Some of the sites were fortified, and all had similar material characteristics. In addition, the northern sites represented a movement to the "limit of aboriginal maize horticulture."[3] Because a consistent pattern of fortifications was lacking, the villagers' occupation of the territory seems to have met with little resistance, at least initially. Later, however, fortifications became more numerous, perhaps indicating a shift in relationships with surrounding groups or the appearance of migrants who were hostile and aggressive.

By about 1400 the territory contracted and village size had increased.

The village distribution became constricted to less than a hundred miles between the Cannonball and the Knife Rivers in North Dakota, and there was a "parallel . . . grouping in much larger and correspondingly better fortified settlements."[4] Some of these villages included as many as a hundred earth lodges and occupied as little as ten acres of land. There was also evidence of the beginning of a shift from the long-rectangular house style to the four-post round houses that were so familiar in historical times. Furthermore, ceramic evidence suggests that these people had contacts with early Arikara populations to the south.

By about 1600 a further constriction of population had occurred. The later sites, which were near the mouth of the Heart River, were prehistoric and historical Mandan villages, although Mandan predecessors had been on the river for a long time before this date. It is also likely that at least one group of Hidatsas was among these early occupants.[5] Since at least some of the other groups of Hidatsas began arriving on the Missouri from the east in about 1650, it may be that the Mandans were limited in their northward movement by these incoming population groups. Village plazas with earth lodges facing the center developed at this time, and the shift from rectangular to circular lodge types may have occurred during this period.

At about the time when some of the Hidatsa groups were arriving on the Missouri, the effects of other social processes were probably also being felt. One of these processes involved the separation of some groups of Hidatsas from the groups on the Missouri River. The separated groups drifted toward the west and became the Crows. While the Crow groups may have begun to become linguistically differentiated from the Hidatsa stock as early as five centuries ago, their gradual geographical separation probably came sometime later, perhaps during the seventeenth century.[6]

An understanding of Mandan and Hidatsa origin traditions is essential for interpreting the role that religion played in their emergence as distinct groups. These traditions gave them a deep sense of place, identity, and continuity with past generations. As we saw in the last chapter, the traditions formed the basic symbolic structures that deeply qualified the way objects, events, and other human and nonhuman beings were experienced in the everyday world. Often two levels are discernible in the origin traditions. On one level, there was the greater tradition of the group, which included its narratives of origin, its creator and culture hero stories, and its normative moral sensibilities. Sometimes these traditions were under the custodial care of one or more religious specialists. On another level, there were smaller traditions generated by kin-based groups and creative individuals. These narratives reflected not only aspects of the greater tradition but also dimensions that arose as a consequence of creative additions. At the level of the greater tradition, religious dimensions dealt with figures who were viewed as more than human and were understood to have shaped the world in fundamental ways. While Mandan and Hidatsa traditions were rich in such material, they also contained echoes of a more recent past. Some of the images reflected a time when they were moving toward their homelands on the Missouri River.

The origin traditions were complex in other ways as well, since they arose among groups that were linguistically related but that had slightly different cultural backgrounds. The Mandans thought that at some time in the past they had been divided into five bands that differed from one another in both culture and dialect. These differences did not constitute fundamentally separate groups, however. As a consequence of historical processes of fusion and assimilation, their social organization was reduced to three major divisions: the Nuptadis, the Nuitadis, and the Awigaxas. After the smallpox epidemic of the eighteenth century, the Awigaxas were assimilated into the Nuitadis. The linguistic differences between the two remaining groups were recognized and recorded by Maximilian during his 1832 visit to Mandan country.[7] In addition, the reduction in the number of separate groups was historically accompanied by a change in the number of villages from perhaps nine or more to two villages associated with the Nuptadi and Nuitadi divisions.[8]

In spite of the cultural differences between the Nuptadis and the Nuitadis, they both had two major origin accounts, which varied somewhat in the telling but which maintained important core elements that were widely shared and that are important for the analysis of religion. One of these traditions (which may have arisen more recently) held that the Mandans were created at the Heart River, a place that from then on had the significance of the center or heart of the world. The other tradition (which may be older) focused on the experiences of the people as they migrated toward the Missouri River from the southeast. A study of the core symbols that characterized the two traditions will aid in understanding the role religion played in the emergence and maintenance of the Mandan identity as a people.

While many traditions were widely known in Mandan society, they were preserved in the memorial tradition by individuals, usually male, who had achieved religious and social visibility. They became the caretakers of the detailed versions of the origin traditions and were in a real sense the oral historians and curators of the people's identity. One such person was White Calf, and his version of the origin tradition is the one we will follow.[9]

In this tradition, the Mandan creator figure, Lone Man, was represented as walking on the surface of primal waters that covered the entire earth. Even though Lone Man was both the creator and the one who originated important cultural institutions, he was portrayed as a being who was uncertain of his own identity. The religious mystery of human origin and destiny was symbolically wrapped in another mystery of a creator who struggled with the question of his own origin. The mystery deepened as Lone Man came upon a plant resting on the water. On the plant was a flower smeared with blood. Speaking a language the creator could understand, the flower said, "My son, you were born from me. I gave birth to you in order that you could go around in the world and do much work."[10]

The deep association of human and greater-than-human beings with the plant world was clearly represented in this tradition. In an even more remarkable manner, the creator was portrayed as dependent for his existence on a plant. The religious roots of the Mandan dependence on plant persons are clearly exposed in these images. This core element of their identity as a people was evoked and sustained by this and the other creation narratives that circulated among them.

The people's association with animal life occurred in this creation account as well. Water birds brought up earth from below the primal sea and assisted the creator in other fundamental ways to prepare the world for the coming of the human beings. In some Mandan versions, there was also an association with the buffalo and with tobacco. In one version the world was created from earth that two ducks brought up. Then the creator fashioned a pipe out of wood taken from a tree that he had created, and tobacco was provided through the agency of a bull buffalo.

As the creator traveled across the earth, he met another person. This was Coyote, who became known in Mandan narratives as First Man. First Man and Lone Man argued about which one was the older. Each bet that he was older than the other. This wager required First Man to remain on the ground lying beside Lone Man's lance.[11] While First Man lay there, Lone Man continued on his way for many years. Returning finally to the place were First Man lay, Lone Man found only scattered bones, but when he took his lance from the ground, First Man leaped up alive, winning the bet and proving that he was the older (and thus the most powerful) of the two. These transcendent predecessors formed the land, with Lone Man making the country on the east of the Missouri River and First Man making the country on the west side of the river.

By the time the land had been completed, there were human beings (Mandans) on it, and Lone Man determined that he would be born among these people. In some versions, Lone Man took the form of a grain of corn that a young woman—often a virgin—ate and through this act became impregnated. In other versions, Lone Man took the form of buffalo kidney fat that a young woman ate, with the same result. According to some versions of the tradition, the child who was born was marked in a special manner, indicating his unique association with the people. This version of Mandan origins also associated the people with a place viewed as the heart of the world. In a tradition narrated by Bear on the Flat, the world was portrayed as a great earth lodge, and the mouth of the Heart River was represented as the fireplace, the burning center from which all life flowed.[12] This tradition formed the symbolic lens through which the people saw their origins and provided the basis for their experience of the landforms that surrounded them.

The second Mandan origin tradition told of the emergence of the people from under the ground at a point on the Mississippi River where it emptied into the Gulf of Mexico. This description follows the account provided by Wolf Chief, a Hidatsa, who received the tradition from his Mandan father-in-law.[13] By the time this version was recorded, Wolf Chief had experienced the vicissitudes of early-twentieth-century reservation life. Nevertheless, he still preserved a memory, albeit mediated, of a tradition that formed earlier Mandan sensibilities about the world.

The chief of the ancient Mandans was known as Good Furred Robe, and he was accompanied by two brothers, Cornhusk Earrings and Uses His Head for Rattle, as well as by a sister, Waving Corn Silk. These four were the children of Corn Father, who, by performing the appropriate rituals, was able to make corn germinate and grow. He was at the end of the line of people who were ascending to the surface of the earth by means of a grape-vine. Corn Father became separated from his children when the vine was broken by the weight of a pregnant woman. Calling to his children from the depths of the earth, Corn Father instructed them to perform all of the rituals they had learned from him.[14]

The Mandans had no trouble integrating the details of these two versions and did not see them as either inconsistent or contradictory. Alfred Bowers, an interpreter of Mandan culture, said, for example,

> My informants did not consider this [the two versions of origin] to be an in-consistency at all. Their explanation was that, when Lone Man made the land around the Heart River, he also made the land to the south as far as the ocean. He made fish people, eagle people, bear people, corn people, buffalo people, and others whose history was inaugurated into myths of the sacred bundles. These various people were born into the Mandan tribe by magical means, thus populating the lands.[15]

Like that constructed by the Mandans, the symbolic universe created by Hidatsa origin traditions was a dynamic reality that developed over time. The traditions also exhibited internal differences related to the separate cultural histories of the three divisions: the Hidatsas proper, the Awaxawis, and the Awatixas. Despite the variations among these traditions, a core embedded in shared symbols persisted relatively unchanged across generations. W. Raymond Wood describes these origin and migration traditions as "rather consistent in content: in spite of the diversity of sources from which the statements were collected, for the most part we are apparently dealing with a single, tenacious cultural tradition, carefully preserved in the oral traditions of the group."[16]

The Awatixa division of the Hidatsas had the longest traditional residence on the Missouri River. It was from this group that the Mountain Crows separated and moved to the west. The next division to arrive on the river was the Awaxawis, and the last to arrive from the east were the Hidatsas proper, from whom the River Crows separated and moved toward the west.[17] The situation may have been even more complex, because the Hidatsa and Crow bands may have been separate groups that migrated to the Plains from their previous homelands.[18] Despite these complexities, it is still possible to describe the symbolic universes that gave rise both to the religious experience and the social identity of the Hidatsas who remained on the river.

In an origin tradition associated with the Hidatsas proper and the Awaxawis, First Creator (Coyote) fashioned the earth out of mud brought to the surface by a diving bird. In later versions, influenced by association with the Mandans, Lone Man appeared along with First Creator. They questioned their own origins, argued over who was older, fashioned the earth on each side of the river, and created animal and human beings.[19] Some of these traditions contained formal elements, such as the image of a creation in six days, that probably indicate later missionary influence.[20]

A prominent Hidatsa woman, Buffalo Bird Woman, told of the people's emergence from beneath Devil's Lake (in present-day northeastern North Dakota) by climbing on a vine. Typically, the vine was broken by the weight of a pregnant woman. Only a part of the group reached the surface, while a number of the people remained below the surface of the waters. According to some Hidatsas, the drums of these underwater villagers were still heard from time to time. After their emergence, the people made their way to the Missouri River, where they met the Mandans.[21] Buffalo Bird Woman also provided the view that the creator's first name was Female Earth, and this being was responsible for making the south side of the Missouri River country warm and soft. The creator's second name was First Worker, according to her recollection.[22] Additional elements concerning the migrations of the people, including references to a celestial fire and a flood, appear in other versions of this tradition.[23]

The Hidatsas proper, the River Crows, and the Awaxawis probably shared the core symbols of the traditions discussed above. By contrast, the Awatixa claimed a separate tradition. According to Bowers, this narrative accounted for "the origin of many ceremonies, most of which began on the Missouri in a restricted area between the Knife and Heart Rivers."[24] The Awatixa tradition, related by Wolf Chief, evoked the symbolism of a culture hero who came down from the sky to establish villages on the earth.[25] According to this tradition, thirteen sky clans were living in earth lodge villages stretching from the zenith to each horizon. While living in this place, the culture hero heard the bellowing of buffaloes. He looked through a hole in the sky and saw buffaloes below on the earth. Since the culture hero was an arrow person, he descended to the earth in this form, landing beside a creek near the present town of Washburn, North Dakota. There Arrow Man met another person, who was able to set the prairies on fire with his flaming ankles. Since this being was threatened by the appearance of another powerful person, he started a fire that charred the body of Arrow Man. As a result, the culture hero became known as Charred Body, and the name of the creek beside which he landed became known as Charred Body Creek. Charred Body defeated the man with flaming ankles, and the earth was thus prepared for the migration of the sky clans. Charred Body selected the most worthy of the arrow beings to come to earth and establish thirteen villages.[26]

After his arrival on earth, Charred Body visited a village of earth Indians in order to court a chief's daughter. The young woman rejected him, and in his rage Charred Body killed her. As a consequence of this deed, a conflict broke out between the earth Indians and the sky Indians, and the tradition expanded to include other important persons. One of these individuals was Charred Body's sister. She survived the conflict between the earth and sky Indians by hiding in a food cache and thus escaping the flames that burned her village. She was pregnant and alone for a time, and one day an evil being, Man With No Head, came to her lodge. In a gesture of hospitality, the young woman set food before him, but Man With No Head said that he could not eat unless he consumed his food in a certain manner. He requested that the young woman lie down and allow her abdomen to be used as a table. Suddenly Man With No Head attacked her, ripped twins from her dying body and threw one of the boys into a spring and the other to the edge of the lodge. Then he propped the woman up, formed a smile on her face, and left the lodge.[27]

The woman's twin boys, Lodge Boy and Spring Boy, clearly had special powers. They matured quickly, and after passing through a ritual process that involved the transformation of Spring Boy from a water being (which he had become) into an Indian, they began to exercise their more-than-human powers. Spring Boy performed an arrow ritual that brought his mother back to life. Then the two young men proceeded to drive other harmful powers from the land. They were so successful in their exploits that they received new names. From this point on they were known as Two Men, and they moved about the land freely, being protected by their powerful arrows.

The leader of the remaining sky people was named Long Arm. He was angered because Two Men had destroyed so many of the beings who possessed sky powers. Long Arm overcame the power of Two Men's arrows and captured Spring Boy, taking him above to the sky land for punishment. Through the renewed power of the arrows, Lodge Boy returned to the sky country and freed his brother, capturing Long Arm's powerful ax as well. As Two Men were about to make their escape, Long Arm tried to prevent them by blocking the hole in the sky with his arm. Two Men threatened to cut off Long Arm's hand if he would not allow them to pass. Defeated, Long Arm agreed to transfer the ritual of the Sun Dance, or Naxpike, to them if they would promise not to use the power of the ax against the sky people.

Now that the tradition had accounted for the origin of the Naxpike, other important events unfolded. In order to transfer the ritual to the earth Indians, Two Men decided to have a "son." This part of the tradition reflected the Hidatsa practice of transfers of power and ritual objects from father to son. Two Men caused a virgin to become pregnant, and Unknown Man was born among the people. He also possessed the power of the arrows, and after proving himself in the traditional manner through success in hunting and war, as well as through a successful marriage, Two Men transferred the ritual of the Sun Dance to the people through their son.

These various origin traditions became associated in both Mandan and Hidatsa experience with a number of female figures. In Hidatsa traditions, Village Old Woman was represented as existing in the beginning. She was apparently equal in power to First Creator and Lone Man because, after they had created the earth and all of the male animals, she created the female animals of all the species: "For each species of living males created by the other two culture heroes, she created females to serve as gods as well as food for the people who were to inhabit the earth."[28] Village Old Woman caused herself to enter into the womb of a young Hidatsa woman, and she was born into the group. In this manner the tradition identified her at a basic symbolic level with the identity and destiny of the people. She also created other transcendent female figures: the Holy Women of the groves of the four directions, another class of beings known simply as the Holy Women, and Woman Above.[29] In Hidatsa experience, Village Old Woman, the Holy Women of the groves of the four directions, and the Holy Women were viewed as beneficent powers.

Woman Above, by contrast, was viewed as a vengeful, dangerous being. Associated symbolically with death, she and her brother, Sun, were cannibals. In a strikingly imaginative manner, the Hidatsa religious universe combined the experience of the everyday world with dimensions of transcendent meaning. In the everyday world of ordinary experience, dead bodies, whether of humans or animals, were observed to rot. The flesh disintegrated and only the bones remained. What better explanation of this observation than the view that the dissolution of the flesh was a consequence of the cannibalistic activities of Sun and his sister, Woman Above?

The Mandans and Hidatsas came to share these traditions and integrated them into their oral cultures. In addition, they shared a tradition that dealt with another powerful female figure, the Old Woman Who Never Dies: "The Hidatsa thought of her as the custodian of all vegetation that ripens or sheds its leaves and is 'rejuvenated' in the spring."[30] In addition, the corn spirits went to live in her lodge during the winter and were sent back to the people with the water birds in the spring. The rhythms of the yearly migrations of these great birds were symbolically associated with the nurture of the people and with their fundamental plant food. With the unification of these traditions in the Mandan and Hidatsa symbolic universes, Old Woman Who Never Dies came to play the role of a goddess of all vegetation, particularly the garden products upon which the people depended.

The Old Woman Who Never Dies tradition embodied some of the cultural meanings that informed female symbolism in Mandan and Hidatsa societies. In an account provided by a Mandan woman named Good Bear,[31] the Old Woman Who Never Dies lived on an island in a great ocean located somewhere below the Cannonball River. Two young men, Black Medicine and Sweet Medicine, discovered her after they were blown to her island by a strange wind. Old Woman greeted them warmly upon their arrival, and they entered her lodge for a meal. She fed them corn mush, which they ate from a pot with clamshell spoons. After they had satisfied their hunger, the pot remained full. The two young men then went outside to hunt. They killed two deer, butchered them, and left the carcasses at the door of the Old Woman's lodge so that she could dry the meat. When they had gone into the lodge, the Old Woman spoke to the deer meat, and the living animals leaped up and ran into the woods. Before they ran off, the Old Woman instructed them to tell the other deer not to come near her lodge since the two young men were such good hunters.

One day in the fall, the narrative continued, the Old Woman told the two young men to keep out of sight since she was about to have important visitors. Even though they obeyed her wish, the young men were still in a position to see what was happening. When the migrating water birds appeared over the island, the boys saw that they were accompanied by corn spirits, who entered the Old Woman's lodge in pairs. Each corn spirit took the form of a beautiful young woman. As they entered the lodge, they deposited gifts of meat at the feet of the Old Woman, saying, "I have come from the northland with your messengers who have shown me the way. Take good care of me or I will die." [32] After the Old Woman agreed to take care of each of the corn spirits and promised to send them back in the spring to the Heart River Mandans, the young women turned into ears of variously colored seed corn—red, blue, yellow, white, pink, black, or a mixed color. Observing all these things, the young men knew that the winter home of the corn spirits was with the Old Woman Who Never Dies and that it was she who sent their spirits back to the people at the time of the spring migration of the great water birds.

The Old Woman was represented in this tradition as a mistress of the animals, having the power to supply hunters with game or to withhold it. She was also presented as a goddess of agriculture, as suggested already by the corn mush that she was cooking when she was discovered by the two young men. This tradition not only mediated important images of female energy and power but also portrayed the relationship between Old Woman and the basic sources of the flourishing and continuance of life. The Mandans' and Hidatsas' identities, as well as their picture of the world, were shaped in fundamental ways by the traditions of the Old Woman Who Never Dies.

The origin traditions of both the Mandans and the Hidatsas were evolving narratives. The stratum of memory represented in these traditions portrayed peoples who had achieved a solid identity, but at the same time these traditions preserved a sense of the separate cultural histories of the various groups. It is also important to understand that social identity emerged as a consequence of intentional acts of interpretation and reinterpretation within shared oral traditions. The Mandans and Hidatsas became who they were through a process of cultural development, and there were probably some individuals and perhaps even some groups who did not come to share these identities. (The split between the Crows and the Hidatsas illustrates this point.) The symbolic boundaries constituting identity thus were not impermeable but rather allowed for the movement of some people through these cultural membranes into another identity, another life. Religious traditions were primary sources of images of the world and of explanations of social origins that formed the permeable yet powerful boundaries that marked the identity of particular groups. These were religious worlds of meaning, rich with particular content and specific to the experience of the groups within which they took form. The next chapter takes up the more particular issue of how these traditions informed important ritual processes, such as the Mandan Okipa and the Hidatsa Naxpike, or Hidebeating ceremony, and became narrative foundations for important bundles.

4 ˅ ˅ ˅ ˅ ˅

Religious Organizations and Ritual Processes

The religious traditions introduced in the last chapter were embodied in social structures and ritual processes that enacted them in the world and that formed the context for understanding their religious meaning. The Okipa was a major societal ritual among the Mandans, while for the Hidatsas the Naxpike, or Hidebeating, ritual was a central religious celebration. Bundles that had significance for the good of the entire society occupied prominent places in these ritual processes. They were gifts from transcendent culture heroes, and the enactment of their rituals maintained and renewed the people's sense of social identity.

The Mandan Okipa was a dense symbolic landscape that embodied many of the people's identity-forming traditions.[1] This ritual was also one of the most widely shared religious practices that related the people to the basic realities that sustained their lives. When the ritual was observed near Fort Clark in the 1830s, the Mandan village was composed of earth lodges arranged around a central plaza. The lodges were from thirty to sixty feet in diameter, and each housed from twenty to thirty persons. The village was surrounded by a stockade and a ditch, and was built so that the border on one side was formed by a high bank rising above the Missouri River.

The ritual observed in the early nineteenth century represented the latest stage in a long process of religious development. The Okipa embodied the entire history of the Mandan people, and its narratives concerned the creation of the earth, animals, plants, and people.[2] Some aspects of these traditions formed a terrain of secret knowledge among the Mandans, and only those who had been involved in the ritual had the authority to relate these portions. Because this knowledge was socially distributed to only a relatively small number, this group became an important locus of social status and power in Mandan society. Those outside this circle could purchase the services of a member of this group to relate aspects of the tradition, but they did not have the right themselves to tell the stories. Furthermore, secret aspects of traditions that formed the text of the Okipa were articulated in an ancient dialect that was understood only by those who had performed leadership roles in the ritual.[3]

The Okipa ceremony was believed to be essential for the good of the entire society and was performed at least once each year. The ritual was initiated by an individual who had had a vision of buffaloes singing Okipa songs. The visionary related his experience to those who had participated in the ritual. If in their judgment the individual was able to endure the required physical and material sacrifices, his vision would be legitimated by the group. If the vision was judged inappropriate, the individual's experience was not credited as sufficient to the task, and he would not be allowed to join those who possessed the secrets and power that accompanied possession of important ritual knowledge.[4]

The major roles in the Okipa were occupied by persons representing Lone Man and Hoita, the Speckled Eagle. There were also singers, the pledger of the ritual, and a number of people who played the part of animals in the various dances that occurred in the course of the ritual. There was also a bundle that contained all the objects and clothing used in the ceremony by the person performing the role of Lone Man. One primary bundle and a number of secondary bundles contained objects that were identical to those in the primary bundle. The owners of these bundles were responsible for caring for the Okipa lodge, the turtle drums, and the cedar at the center of the plaza, which represented Lone Man.[5]

The Okipa lodge reminded the people of Dog Den Butte, where, early in their history, Hoita had imprisoned all of the animals. In a version of this tradition related by White Calf, Hoita is said to have been living among the Mandans.[6] At this time Lone Man caused himself to be born among the people, and when he became a young man he had an important conflict with Hoita. Lone Man wanted one of Hoita's white robes, and he was able to secure the help of powerful sky beings to accomplish his purpose. After unsuccessful attempts by Thunder, Rain, and Sun to get the robe, Whirlwind was finally able to blow it away. When the robe was found far to the north by a group of Mandans, they returned it to the village and presented it to Lone Man. Hoita was angered and took all of the animals with him to Dog Den Butte. The Okipa dances embodied part of the tradition that told about how Lone Man secured the release of the animals from Hoita.

The Okipa lasted for four days and began with an announcement by a ceremonial leader that an important event was about to happen. This announcement was made from the roof of an earth lodge before sunrise, and in response the members of the village gathered excitedly on top of the lodges to await the sunrise and the beginning of the ritual that was about to unfold. Just as the sun was rising, a figure appeared in the west and approached the village. Met by a group of warriors, this strange figure told them that he had come to open the Okipa lodge. The important men of the village gathered, their faces painted black, and they immediately recognized the stranger as Lone Man. This person was dressed in a robe made of four white wolf skins, and he was painted with white clay over his entire body. After opening the lodge, Lone Man requested that four men, symbolizing the cardinal directions, prepare the lodge for the ritual. During the remainder of the day the lodge was cleaned and decorated with willows and various herbs. While the lodge was being prepared, Lone Man visited every earth lodge, relating the traditions of origin to the people and telling of the time when he had been born among them.

The next morning Lone Man called together all of the men who were to endure suffering in the Okipa lodge. These men were painted variously in red, white, yellow, blue, or green. Each carried a bow, a shield, and his personal medicine bundle. In single file they followed Lone Man into the lodge. The interior of the lodge contained a number of interesting symbolic objects. There were rattles, turtle drums, four buffalo skulls, and four human skulls, which evoked the memory of Good Furred Robe, his brothers, and sister. The young men participating in the torture features of the ritual remained within the Okipa lodge for four days without eating or drinking.

The turtle drums were originally believed to have been acquired by Lone Man. According to a tradition related by Scattercorn, a woman whose father had assumed the identity of Hoita, the drums used in the Okipa were first made of buffalo hide. Because worms came out of this hide when it was beaten, Lone man sought a better alternative. He asked Beaver, then Badger, and finally Otter to become the drums in the ceremony, but none of these animals were strong enough to endure being beaten by the drumsticks. Lone Man's search for Okipa drums led him finally to an ocean, where he found a large turtle lying on the bottom. This turtle was actually supporting the world on his back, and thus he could not leave his post to accompany Lone Man back to the Mandan villages. But Turtle said, "You can look me over and make your drums just like me." [7] Lone Man returned to the Mandans and constructed four drums like turtles out of thick buffalo hide. After they were completed, the drums were alive. One of them took offense because he was decorated with feathers that he did not like. This turtle returned to the water, so only three drums remained for use in the Okipa ritual.

During the four days of the Okipa, an important animal dance took place in the center of the plaza. The participants danced four times on the first day, eight on the second, twelve on the third, and sixteen on the fourth day. They were dressed in buffalo skins with the head and tail attached, and the men peered out from the eyes of the buffalo, which they came to resemble as the ritual unfolded. These dancers were arranged in pairs and positioned themselves at the four principal directions of the plaza. Joining them were four additional men, two of whom were painted black, symbolizing night, and two red, symbolizing light or day. In addition to these figures, there were other pairs of dancers representing important animals and birds in the Mandan environment. The leader of the ritual, carrying a pipe he had received from Lone Man, was painted yellow. Each time the buffalo dance occurred, he brought with him out of the lodge the old men who beat the turtle drums and a man who shook the rattles for the dance. The men who enacted animal roles became, through the ritual, the species they represented, and at the end of each dance session they would respond in their animal voices and with appropriate animal movements. Through the ritual, buffalo and other animal persons actually came dancing among the people, giving them confidence that they would appear again in the hunt, becoming food for the people.

On the fourth day there appeared another figure in the west. This person was painted black "with pulverized charcoal and grease, with rings of white clay over his limbs and body. Indentations of white, like huge teeth, surrounded his mouth, and white rings surrounded his eyes."[8] He carried a rod with a red ball, the end of which he slid along the ground as he ran among the people. The significance of this figure, who like Lone Man appeared from the west but who exhibited Trickster features, was related in a fascinating manner to the renewal of the buffalo. His sexuality was prominent, appearing to all in his gigantic wooden penis, the shaft of which was painted black and the end bright red. Each time this being raised his rod, the enormous penis rose—to the consternation of the women at whom he directed this organ. Only the pipe of Lone Man was able to stop his advance. During the course of the last buffalo dance, this being mounted four of the eight animal figures, fertilizing them in an act of mimetic sexual intercourse.

There was a reversal of gender roles at the end of the buffalo dance. The renewal of the buffalo was symbolically accomplished through a male organ, but in the end, female symbolism was reasserted through the agency of a woman who defeated the Trickster. At the end of the dance, a group of women pursued Trickster and broke his staff, and one of them captured his enormous penis, which she wrapped in sage and brought back to the village. From the top of the Okipa lodge, this woman claimed that "she had the power of creation, and of life and death over them; that she was the father of all the buffaloes, and that she could make them come or stay away as she pleased."[9] Matrilineal power was thus reasserted through a ritual reversal of gender roles. Men did the hunting, to be sure, and men were involved in the activity of fertilizing females, but women were represented as the deeper source of fecundity. This fecundity was symbolically represented as more powerful than the male principle, which, in the person of the Trickster, was overcome by a woman. Also we can see that the woman who captured the

penis interpreted herself as master of the animals, an image that was supported in the oral traditions of the people.

This ritual was followed by one that enacted the renewal of the buffalo in the world in a more dramatic fashion. The woman who defeated the
Trickster became the central figure in this ritual, and in preparation several
old men went throughout the community, shaking rattles and announcing
that "the whole government of the Mandans was then in the hands of one
woman—she who had disarmed the Evil Spirit, and to whom they were to
look during the coming year for buffaloes to supply them with food, and
keep them alive; that all must repair to their wigwams and not show themselves outside; that the chiefs on that night were old women; that they [the
men] had nothing to say." [10]

The ritual took place in the plaza and involved the following participants: the eight men who performed the buffalo dance at the Okipa, the
leader of the Okipa ritual, the drummers and the man who had shaken the
rattle, several old chiefs, and several young married women under the leadership of the woman who had defeated the Trickster. After feeding the men
who were present, the women danced while the men smoked a pipe and
looked on. After the first phase of the dance, the leading woman selected a
man from the group, took him by the arm, and led him outside the village.
The ritual intercourse of Trickster with dancing buffalo became incarnate
in the intercourse between these women and men. At the end of the ritual,
the men involved promised to give liberal gifts and to smoke a pipe of
reconciliation with the husbands, which the husbands were bound by the
norms of the group to accept.

The general fertility symbolism in this ritual was obvious, but the cultural significance among the Mandans was more complex. At one level there
was the notion that power could be transmitted through the act of sexual
intercourse. In this context, the women who had intercourse with the buffalo (men who symbolically had become these beings) were related through
that act to the power of this important animal. Through this means, their
husbands came to share in power that would assure them many successful
hunts. At another level, the enactment of the ritual enabled the participants actually to accomplish, in the universe created by the ritual, the desired end: the reproduction of the buffalo. Through sexual acts the buffalo

were actually reproduced. These acts did not "represent" fertilization, but rather, within the Mandan symbolic universe, they were believed to produce the desired consequences. At still another level, sexual intercourse between these women and the buffalo men established a kinship between the people and the animal upon which they depended for food.[11]

Induced suffering was also an important part of the Okipa ritual. Through suffering, individuals increased their spiritual capital and sought to insure greater social influence. Male participants in the Okipa, including the ones who submitted to torture, had their glans covered by tying their foreskins securely with small strips of deer thong. Then the entire pubic area was smeared with white clay.[12] Given the power associated with sexuality and the sexual organ, it may be that covering the genital area had something to do with preserving the participants from a loss of potency during the ritual.

After continuing their fast into fourth day, the young men presented themselves to two men, one of whom made incisions and the other of whom inserted skewers into the flesh. Cuts were made on their chest, shoulders, arms, and legs. Then the sufferers were suspended by thongs tied to the chest or back skewers. In addition, buffalo skulls hung from skewers inserted into their arms and legs. After the men were raised about three or four feet above the ground, a man with a long stick began to spin the sufferer, slowly at first but then faster and faster until the person fainted, his head hung down, and often his tongue protruded from his mouth. Then, one observer said, "When brought to this condition, without signs of animation, the lookers-on pronounced the word *dead! dead!*"[13]

After this part of their ordeal was over, each sufferer presented himself to a man whose body was painted red and his hands and feet black, and who wore a mask. After offering a finger to transcendent persons, the masked figure cut off the little finger of their left hand. In some instances the sufferer immediately offered the forefinger of the same hand, which was cut off in the same manner. An even greater sacrifice, done by a few, was to offer the little finger of the right hand. A final aspect of the torture ritual was the "last race." Young men ran around the plaza, dragging buffalo skulls that hung from skewers in their arms and legs until these objects were torn away from their flesh. After healing, these wounds would leave their mark, reminding all who saw their bodies that they had endured important suffering, had deepened their spiritual experience, and for these reasons possessed honorable scars.[14]

The Okipa ritual demonstrates that this was a society that valued bodily privation and sacrifice. While it is true that significant wounds that produced appropriate scarification were badges of social status and generated social acceptance, it is possible that suffering was considered necessary to assure the life and well-being of the entire group. Suffering was a form of religious action that was deeply routinized in these societies and was informed by the belief that this action would evoke the desired responses from important transcendent persons and powers.

The Okipa of the historical Mandans certainly had some continuity with the prehistoric predecessors of these people, although the ritual forms would have evolved as the villages shifted from largely dispersed settlements to more cohesive units. What is clear about the historical ritual is that it embodied and maintained in the experience of the people some of their primary identity-forming traditions. Long before the early nineteenth century, the Mandans had become a people, and performing the Okipa was essential to their remaining a people. It mediated the major traditions that recalled their creation, migration, and settlement on the Missouri, and it included as well the presence of their culture hero, Lone Man. The ritual renewed the reservoirs of memory that were so important for their sense of identity and of continuity in their experience.

It is also clear that the ritual process of the Okipa was one of the world-building activities that gave structure to the Mandans' experience of the everyday world. The yearly unfolding of the ritual gave rise to a shared experience of the surrounding territory as the heart of the world. These webs of meaning were grounded in memories that transcended the group, and when embodied in the Okipa ritual they recalled the activities of Lone Man, who gave rise to the group as a separate people.

In addition to the Okipa, other ritual processes were deeply connected with the growth of plants and their cultivation. Among the Mandans, these rituals were associated with major bundles that were believed to have originated as a consequence of the activities of Good Furred Robe. The Good Furred Robe tradition was enacted in the rituals of two important bundles. The Robe bundle contained Good Furred Robe's pipe and robe, and the

Skull bundle contained the skulls identified with the culture hero and his brothers.[15] The enactment of the rituals associated with these bundles was the responsibility of the Corn Priests, whose office in early times was hereditary and continued for the life of the person. The outcome of their actions was viewed as absolutely critical for a successful growing season and harvest.

The Corn Priest engaged in other important activities as well.[16] Before planting time he prepared corn kernels, a few of which he distributed to each of the women. When mixed with their seed corn, the fecundity of their crops was believed to be ensured—if the Corn Priest correctly performed his other ritual work. This work began after the seed had been planted. The priest painted his body daily and wore the same clothes, including a winter buffalo robe. In addition, he was not permitted to bathe during the entire period. In the course of the growing season, this individual performed garden rituals and only returned to the activities of his ordinary life after the corn was ripe.

In addition, the Corn Priest performed important rituals at the time when corn was traded to other groups: "It was thought that it [the ritual] must be done or the spirits in the corn might leave the Mandan and help the people who took the corn away. He [the Corn Priest] dressed in his ceremonial outfit and 'called back' the Corn Spirits."[17] In addition to this important activity, the Corn Priest performed an essential role in selecting sites for new villages. Such a choice had fundamental consequences for the group, since it was imperative that villages be located in areas where the soil and other conditions supported productive gardening.[18]

These Mandan bundles and ritual processes were clearly intertwined with the way social status and power were understood by the people. Inheritance patterns for major bundles proceeded along the line of the matrilineal clan, and a great deal of social control was exercised in the process. As a consequence, the keepers of major bundles occupied an important position in the village power structure. Not only were they responsible for ritual processes that were essential to the life of the people but they were also expected to endure considerable personal sacrifice in the performance of their ritual work.[19]

A discussion of the Naxpike,[20] or Hidatsa Hidebeating ritual (referred to by some interpreters as a Sun Dance), will provide a comparative context for deepening our understanding of religious organizations and ritual processes among the village societies. While it is perhaps true that among the Plains Indians the Sun Dance was an "anthropological invention,"[21] at least in the sense that it became an interpretive construct that sometimes concealed complex differences among rituals, some significant similarities did develop among the various ritual processes on the Northern Plains.[22] The core of many of these ritual processes was quite old and embodied a fundamental symbolism connected with group identity. Thus even though similarities with the rituals of other groups appeared at certain levels of the ritual process, the Hidatsa ceremony was distinctive because it was informed by the Charred Body tradition.

In the previous chapter we saw that after their conflict with Long Arm and their capture of his sacred ax, Two Men decided to have a son through the agency of a virgin. When this son, Unknown Man, was mature and had a wife, Two Men came to the village (traditionally identified as Awatixa), transferred power and ritual knowledge to their son, and instructed him in all the details of the Naxpike. Some interpreters viewed Long Arm as the final locus of the powers that came to potency in the Naxpike ritual. It was Long Arm who "instructed Two Men to have the ceremony performed by their son [Unknown Man] in order that the supernatural powers for success in hunting and warfare possessed by Two Men would be transmitted to the Hidatsa by means of the sacred arrows and sacred ax."[23] This shared narrative embodied meanings associated with a bundle and a ritual. It was through this living bundle and its ritual enactment that the reality of the tradition was reinforced, the potency of the bundle was made actual, and social power, gender relations, and status were legitimated in the Hidatsa world.

The Naxpike and the Long Arm bundle evolved over a considerable period. When observers gathered information about the ritual, the social complexity and derived status relations they described were thus products of a long social process. Even though the details of this development are largely unrecoverable, the complexities of the ritual are interesting, and they illustrate how the Naxpike functioned in Hidatsa society. By the nineteenth century, rather than a single Long Arm bundle there were several bundle lines, all of which were believed to have originated with Unknown Man.[24] This founding tradition legitimated a number of social processes related to the bundles.

A system of ritual knowledge was the center of the social process that involved a transfer of bundles from father to son. Even though bundles were believed to be alive, they could be and were duplicated.[25] A father could transfer his ritual knowledge along with a bundle to successive sons four times, although transfers probably occurred fewer than four times. With each transfer, a new bundle would be created by the father, or a member of the father's clan if the father was no longer living. Even though a bundle was transferred, a father retained his rights to the ritual knowledge and participation in the Naxpike. Since residence was matrilocal, the father and his married son were of different clans. For this reason, the transfer of a bundle involved a shift in the family locus of ritual objects and knowledge. But because the father retained his ritual rights, a social link was created between the various clans.

What emerges from this picture is a complex system that enables the transfer of social status and power. Because the founding tradition established the Hidatsa social identity and mediated powers relating to important group activities such as hunting and warfare, custodial care and sharing in ritual knowledge and practice carried the empirical benefits of social status and power. Because the fathers, while alive, retained a share in the religious knowledge and ritual process, social power tended to accumulate in groups of older males. But the transfer process involved a shift in clan location for the bundles and limited the degree to which social power could be monopolized over long periods by particular family groups.

A person was viewed as socially qualified to perform the Naxpike not only on the basis of his father's relation to a bundle but also on the basis of certain personal characteristics and spiritual experiences. The individual must have demonstrated that he could undergo the physical privations as well as bear the economic burdens of the ritual, and he needed to be in a stable marriage, since his wife or wives assisted him in the preparations for the ritual and the ritual itself. In practice, these restrictions meant that he would usually be socially mature, probably having reached the age of around thirty before he became qualified to perform the ritual.

In addition, the individual must have undergone vision and/or dream experiences having to do with the People Above, which then had to be socially legitimated by the older males of his father's clan. In Hidatsa society there were instances of young men who had the right by inheritance to perform the ritual but who never had appropriate dreams. Given these restrictions, it is clear that the older males who provided the interpretation of young men's dreams possessed considerable social power. They were gatekeepers who controlled access to ritual knowledge that brought highly desired social recognition and power.

Since a number of these Naxpike bundle lines existed and since there was a community of male kinspersons of various ages who shared either in taking care of the bundle or in its ritual knowledge, some interpreters have viewed these bundle owners as members of "fraternities."[26] When the Hidatsas located at Like-a-Fishhook village in 1845, all of the bundles but one were understood to have equal status. The exception was the Naxpike bundle associated with Awatixa village, which contained Long Arm's sacred ax. This bundle was superior to the others in status and function. Whenever the Naxpike was enacted at Like-a-Fishhook village, the individual who ritually became Long Arm and exercised the power of the sacred ax in the ritual was the caretaker of the bundle at Awatixa village.[27]

Preparations for the Naxpike involved both a gathering of property and a focusing of social energy. After an individual's vision experiences were interpreted by the appropriate group, a web of socially legitimated obligations began to structure the activities of a number of other individuals and groups. The members of the pledger's clan, his relatives, and the men in his age society were expected to assist in the gathering of goods to be used as gifts. The relatives and clan members of the pledger's wife, and the members of her age society were also expected to contribute generously. The pledger was expected to focus his attention on successful hunting in order to acquire a large number of hides, which, when tanned, would be given along with other goods to those who officiated in the ritual process.[28] The gathering of property and the focusing of energy was done for the sake of enacting the drama of the relationship between Long Arm and Two Men. This ritual reproduced the power and social benefits associated with these figures and, at the center, was the symbolism of the sacred arrows.

As was true for many other rituals among peoples on the Northern Plains who shared what became known as the Sun Dance, the Naxpike required a structure that would become the locus of the ritual process. Building this structure involved the activities of other groups in Hidatsa society. The required social division of labor included not only the males but also females and a class of men who were differently gendered in Hidatsa society, the berdaches. The Holy Women's society was responsible for the preparation of the area where the Naxpike was to be held, and a number of berdaches were assigned to assist in digging the hole for the center pole. One of the berdaches was also responsible for the selection of the center pole. A berdache was involved in preparations for the Crow Sun Dance as well, which is not surprising, given the fact that the people who became the Crows once shared with the Hidatsas an identity and a social world.[29]

The center pole itself was a dense symbol, evoking multiple levels of meaning in Hidatsa experience. Two of these meaning complexes were central to the symbolism of the arrows, one dimension of which related to success in warfare and the other to hunting. When the center pole had been selected, young men dressed in their finest clothing and riding their best horses set upon the pole as if it were an enemy. While this motif was shared by other groups on the Northern Plains, it was infused with meanings particular to the Charred Body tradition and the war-making powers that Two Men, who were the sacred arrows, had transferred to the Hidatsas through the Naxpike.[30]

Hunting symbolism was prominent as well, materially evoked by the tying of a buffalo head, which was attached to a strip of skin that included the tail, to the fork in the center pole. This living object evoked in the experience of the people who saw it elements of the Charred Body tradition having to do with the time when the game was sent to the Hidatsas by Two Men. Central to these meanings must have been memories of the figure in the tradition who finally identified himself as Buffalo, a master-of-the-animals figure. This animal person gave instructions to the people concerning appropriate ritual acts and offerings that should be made to the beings upon whom they depended for food.[31]

When completed, the Naxpike lodge included a center pole against which were leaned poles with their leafy branches still attached. The lodge was probably formed in the shape of a conical tipi.[32] Solar, lunar, and astral symbols emblazoned on cloth or hide evoked in the experience of the people the reality of the People Above. It was inside this structure that the drama of the Charred Body tradition unfolded. The major participants were the individuals who, through their ritual actions, *became* Long Arm and Spring Boy. As was true of many other Northern Plains rituals, the Naxpike required four days to complete. During this time the reality of the everyday world was brought into relationship with and interpenetrated by the reality created by the ritual. Central to this reality was the suffering of Spring Boy, who was, in everyday life, the person whose visions had been legitimated by the fathers. The other person, who represented Long Arm, also possessed knowledge essential to the performance of the ritual. This knowledge was not given directly to the pledger but rather was mediated to him through a member of his father's clan, who served as an instructor.

Long Arm painted and dressed Spring Boy in clothing that corresponded with the tradition, and the ritual officially began when Spring Boy danced before the center pole, where the buffalo hide was hung. During the course of four days, Spring Boy and the other fasters underwent the piercing of flesh on each side of their chest. Skewers pushed through these wounds were attached to thongs and then to the center pole. By pulling back against the skewers and swinging around the pole, each participant subjected himself to intense pain, anticipating that as a consequence a powerful dream or vision would occur. For those families who supported the fasters, the expectation was that future hunts would be successful and that they would be victorious over their enemies.

At the close of the ritual, Long Arm, Spring Boy, and his wife or wives were prepared, through songs and by purification in a sweat lodge, to re-enter the world of everyday life. Then the participants were feasted with food prepared by the wives of the man who had ritually become Long Arm. As a consequence of these events, both the individual participants and Hidatsa society received the benefits afforded them through the enactment of symbols that were believed to have profound and socially essential effects in the world of everyday affairs.

Rituals and age societies involving women were also present among the Hidatsas, but because they were similar to those of the Mandans, they are discussed in the next chapter. The discussion here concerns the question of why, despite the pressures of disease and increasing physical proximity, rituals such as the Okipa and the Naxpike were kept relatively intact and distinct from each other, in contrast to other rituals, which became widely shared among both the Mandans and the Hidatsas.

The Okipa and the bundles that derived from the Good Furred Robe tradition embodied transcendent dimensions of Mandan experience, and they were also connected with and gave structure to systems of social status and power at the level of the everyday world. The Hidebeating ritual, which enabled the transfer of the principal bundles, performed similar functions among the Hidatsas. These systems of social organization and power resisted change for a very long time even though both groups experienced many traumas, not the least of which were the great smallpox epidemics. An early-twentieth-century interpreter argued that both the Mandans and the Hidatsas tended to be conservative and unwilling to reveal their religious traditions and practices to outsiders. Furthermore, they attributed their decline as a group to the fact that their predecessors had revealed too much to whites in earlier years.[33]

It is clear that religious traditions and ritual processes were essential features of Mandan and Hidatsa identities, because they gave rise to their respective broader social worlds. Some further exploration of how religious traditions and ritual processes enabled these peoples to adjust their identities and social worlds over time will deepen our understanding of how they responded creatively to the sometimes almost overwhelming pressures that bore down upon them. The next chapter shows how both Mandans and Hidatsas remained distinctive peoples while at the same time changing in response to new circumstances.

5 ▽ ▽ ▽ ▽ ▽

Religious Continuity and Change in the Village Societies

Traditions that informed the Okipa and Naxpike rituals were embodied in powerful symbols, were enacted periodically, and were crucial for the formation of social identity among the Mandans and Hidatsas. These religious traditions and practices drew deep and persistent symbolic boundaries between the groups, boundaries that were preserved in the face of considerable pressure and cultural trauma. The religious universes constituted by these symbolic structures and maintained by their ritual processes not only differentiated one group from the other but also shaped individual identities through the personal experiences that were associated with participation in them.

In addition to participation in societal rituals, individual identity and social location were shaped by additional religious practices and more personal ritual objects. Even though the male pronoun appears in the following text, the following statement could apply to women as well as men, since both participated in religious groups and shared in ritual processes.

> One's ritual possessions were so much a part of his daily life that whenever someone is mentioned, people today recall both his ritual rights and other records. . . . In time, each personal achievement was expressed in terms of the supernatural. These personal records are repeated over and over until they be-

come stylized and differ no more, as told by different individuals, than do the sacred myths relating to the various ceremonies.[1]

Even though these sentiments represented the interpretations of people who were looking back on the religious past of their group, it is still clear that considerable significance was attached to religious participation and religious objects such as bundles. Given these deep roots, it is not difficult to understand some of the social sources of Mandan and Hidatsa religious conservatism. Nevertheless, despite this conservatism, important changes did occur in Mandan and Hidatsa religious traditions and practices as the Mandan and Hidatsa people made constructive responses to particular events. While some of the interpreters reviewed in the first chapter concluded that these events were significant factors in explaining social change, the emphasis here is on cultural *responses* to these events. It was at the level of their religious responses that Northern Plains societies were able to make sense of what was happening to them.

Some parts of the larger context within which the people made their constructive responses need further elaboration, particularly the smallpox epidemic of 1837. The epidemic diseases that devastated peoples along the Missouri River and elsewhere on the Northern Plains were extremely powerful and disorganizing events.[2] Not only were populations decimated but disturbances in the social transmission of ritual knowledge and power occurred as whole bundle lines disappeared in both the Mandan and Hidatsa societies. These epidemics were particularly devastating to the Mandans. Their estimated population in 1750 was about 9,000; after the epidemic of 1837, only about twenty-three adult males, forty adult females, and up to seventy young people remained.[3] In the language of one interpreter of Mandan culture, "extinction is the most devastating and final result of culture contact situations."[4]

But the Mandans did not become extinct. Instead they responded to the devastation of 1837 by employing several measures to stabilize and increase their population. One of these involved the requirement that a man from another group who married a Mandan woman had to agree that any children of the union would speak the Mandan language and that both he and the children would be socialized into the cultural practices and values of the group. Ritual adoption was an additional practice that enabled the population to expand during this critical time. Finally, women captured in warfare were often adopted into Mandan society. As a consequence of these intentional social processes, as well as some natural increase, the Mandan population increased to about 150 after the spring of 1837 and to about 250 by 1862.[5]

Even after the decimation of their population, many important Mandan rituals remained, though some bundle lines had disappeared. Indeed, ritual activity increased as the aggressive impulses of the Mandans were turned against whites and their enemies. They also expanded the practice of self-torture in an effort to obtain power to protect themselves against the collapse of their social and religious universe.[6] The Okipa continued to be enacted until 1889, which clearly indicates the persistence of an important aspect of their religious culture.[7] In commenting on continuing Mandan conservatism, one interpreter writing at the end of the fur trading period said:

> It is somewhat remarkable that notwithstanding all the misfortunes that have befallen this tribe for so many years, it even to this time preserves its independence and individuality as a nation. . . . They will not . . . practice any customs but those of their ancestors. Their religious rites and ceremonies are preserved entire and the system of self-inflicting tortures is practiced at the present day.[8]

The three Hidatsa groups were also severely affected by the 1837 epidemic, although the most serious population reductions occurred among the Awaxawi and Awatixa divisions. Even though the Hidatsas proper were dispersed during some of this time and were less affected, the total picture for the three groups was grim. Bowers claimed, for example, that "a majority of the original tribal council died at that time."[9] Religious and political leadership patterns, ritual knowledge, and bundle lines were affected, but Hidatsa religious culture did not collapse. The Naxpike continued for some years after the epidemic of 1837, the last performance being in 1879, ten years before the last Okipa.

In addition to reducing the Mandan and Hidatsa populations, epidemic diseases also forced a reduction in the number of villages, which brought the groups into even closer physical and cultural proximity. In about 1782, for example, there were perhaps as many as nine Mandan villages on both sides of the Missouri in the vicinity of the mouth of the Heart River.[10] By 1797 the number of villages had been reduced to five.[11] Eighteenth-century reductions in population also weakened the village societies and made them vulnerable to attack from nomadic Siouan groups.

In response to these pressures, the Mandans and Hidatsas sought to re-organize their societies. By the time of the 1837 epidemic, the Hidatsa groups had organized themselves into a loose federation. Each group had a council of headmen, five of whom came from the Hidatsa-proper group, three from the Awatixas, and two from the Awaxawis. The Mandan social organization had come to resemble a theocracy, with the men who had spon-sored the Okipa ritual being the head policy makers and the leader of the corn rituals being responsible for assigning the garden plots. Both the Man-dans and the Hidatsas had by this time also developed a fully functioning group, the Black Mouths, which maintained social order and managed in-tergroup disputes.[12] Intermarriage among the various groups increased, as did the extent of cooperation between villages in the enactment of cere-monies.[13] Even though the major rituals remained distinct, cultural inter-changes in other areas of religious life were surely taking place during this period.

The pressures created by disease and warfare produced a shift in the di-vision of labor and power relations between men and women. In earlier times the dual economy, which was expressed in religious traditions and ritual practices having to do with hunting and agriculture, embodied a divi-sion among males and females that exhibited important reciprocities. Oral traditions and ritual knowledge concerning hunting and agriculture were distributed along gender lines, as were hunting and agricultural bundles. At this earlier stage, social relationships and access to forms of power were more balanced than they became when warfare—a predominantly male activity—became a primary focus of social energies. Not only did males engage in war and acquire social status through such participation, they also were forced to protect the gardens from raids by enemies, displacing women's roles in the process. This shift in power relations may account for an increase in the male ownership of bundles connected with agriculture.

Even though such shifts occurred, the cultural importance of warfare was a recent acquisition and did not completely obscure the older divisions of labor and cultural values in Mandan and Hidatsa society.[14]

An important condition that stimulated social change throughout this period was the increase in intermarriage. Between 1804 and 1862, intermarriage became common among all three Hidatsa groups. Intermarriage between these groups and the Arikaras, however, was minimal.[15] Closer physical proximity and increased intermarriage stimulated the social distribution of knowledge about religious traditions and provided opportunities to observe each other's ritual processes.

Even with the changes introduced by responses to both the earlier epidemic of 1781–82 and the devastation of 1837, Mandan and Hidatsa societies still maintained a great deal of their separate social organization. They preserved rituals and religious traditions that distinguished them from each other despite increased intermarriage and cooperation in the performance of ceremonies. Their respective social identities were not extinguished by the many deaths that resulted from smallpox and other diseases. Rather, they developed a new religious synthesis that provided for continuities in ritual action and cooperation, and maintained core distinctions that supported a sense of identity within each group.

The Mandan Okipa and the Hidatsa Naxpike mediated a special sense of access to power and to religiously grounded values that was believed to be essential for the well-being of both individuals and the group. Even though processes of change were underway, these ritual processes focused on bundles maintained, along with a stock of secret knowledge, by religious elites—the bundle holders. Access to the power and knowledge, as well as to the beneficent consequences of the bundles, continued to be carefully guarded and socially controlled. Robert Lowie described the Hidatsa understanding of these matters:

> The origin of bundles is ascribed to certain experiences with supernatural powers, and their recital is not lightly undertaken. From the native point of view it seems that full knowledge is restricted to the [bundle] fraternity and anyone else retailing what data he has picked up not only necessarily falls into error but stands revealed as a poacher encroaching on alien property rights.[16]

Lowie met considerable resistance when he attempted to get people to reveal to him the contents of a bundle, and even if the bundle was opened, the owner demanded what he deemed to be an exorbitant price. This experience was similar to that reported by visitors to the villages in the 1830s.[17]

Despite such cultural tenacity, changes had been underway in Mandan and Hidatsa societies both before and after European contact. Even after they became involved in the fur trade, however, changes often occurred as a consequence of the operation of factors that were internal to these societies.[18] For this reason, many changes were legitimated by shared cultural practices and were often perceived as a development of their religious and cultural traditions rather than a radical departure from them. In this sense, deeply ingrained cultural practices shaped both the way social changes were interpreted and the form that they took in the society.

One of the cultural features that legitimated social change was the importance placed on dreams.[19] Even though interpretation was socially controlled, dreaming produced a kind of creative instability in the religious culture of the groups. Transcendent others—whether animal, plant, or personified natural processes—approached human beings in ways that were often unexpected. Thus a particular vision experience might break through socially legitimated interpretations and become integrated into the on going religious practices of the group. Further, because dreaming was based on a general human capacity, it was an experience that could not be completely controlled. Anyone at any level of the social structure and people of both genders could dream. This was a source of instability that stimulated change in the Mandan and Hidatsa societies.

The creative instability provided by dreaming was related to supportive features in the religious systems. Bowers said, for example, that "The Hidatsa ceremonial system was 'open at the top' . . . to provide for the occasional introduction of new bundle rites."[20] This openness qualified what was otherwise a conservative structure and made it possible for vision/dream experiences endured by individuals to give rise to new elements in the ritual processes of the group even though there was no wholesale transmission of central religious ceremonies from one group to the other.

Also important for stimulating social change was the widespread practice of ritual adoption. Especially in Hidatsa society, this practice gave rise to the transfer of dances, bundles, and other cultural items. In this case, however, the transfers were often between the Hidatsas and peoples other than the Mandans. Bowers said, for example, that "There were numerous friendships between individual Hidatsas and members of alien bands who customarily came to the villages to trade for corn. In return, a prominent Hidatsa would pledge a return visit at some future date at a rendezvous out on the prairies."[21]

These friendships were sealed by an adoption ritual that often involved the use of a pipe and required that a Hidatsa "father" select for adoption a "son" from another group. Then both the father and the son, along with their families and age-society members, would prepare gifts for exchange at the adoption ritual. An adoption pipe would be made by a specially qualified person, and the Hidatsa father, along with his relatives, would set out bearing gifts to the son in the other society. These Hidatsa parties "went far out onto the prairies even as far as the Black Hills and the Powder River, traveling as an organized group and through territory occupied by unfriendly groups to reach the band where the adoption was to be made."[22]

Social changes introduced through purchase or transfer sometimes appeared among village peoples within the context of the age societies. Such a case was related by Wolf Chief, who was born in about 1849.[23] This transfer occurred in about 1880 or 1881 when a group of Santee Sioux from Devil's Lake passed on a form of the Grass Dance to a group composed of young Mandan and Hidatsa men.[24] This ritual was typical of earlier ones and involved feasting and an exchange of gifts, including horses and other goods. The Sioux instructed the initiates in the details of the dance and transferred to them special dance regalia and ritual objects. According to Wolf Chief, an important part of the ritual was a public declaration of friendship. A Sioux would say before the assembled group, "I want to make so-and-so my friend," delivering to the person his dance outfit. The response of the person would be, "I give you a horse."[25] This ritual, along with the other social processes involved in the transfer, occurred in an earth lodge and was witnessed by male and female members of the respective groups.

Even though some interpreters did not consider the men's age societies as "sacred,"[26] the transfer of the Grass Dance clearly involved conceptions that related to the acquisition of power for male success in war and were thus at least broadly religious. Walking Soldier, a Sioux, said on the occasion of the transfer, "This dance society is a sacred society and we observe it with reverence. When a war party is out they pray to these objects for success."[27] The objects referred to were the headdress, armlets, leggings, bells, skins, and eagle feathers that were a part of the dance outfit. Walking Horse also referred to the promise made by several Sioux men the previous summer, that "if everything went well and was propitious, we would let you have the songs. Now we hear that last winter your young men slew some enemies and that you therefore had rejoicing. We take this to be a favorable sign, and we therefore come to give you the songs."[28] The special power evoked by the dance was essentially related to the songs, the acquisition of which led to success in warfare.[29]

Another feature in village societies that may have been a stimulus for social change was the relative marginality of berdaches and their freedom. Their liminal position may have been a source of religious change in some groups. Among the Hidatsas, for example,

> The berdaches comprised the most active ceremonial class in the village. Their roles in ceremonies were many and exceeded those of the most distinguished tribal ceremonial leaders. There was an atmosphere of mystery about them. *Not being bound as firmly by traditional teachings coming down from the older generations through the ceremonies, but more as a result of their own individual and unique experiences with the supernatural, their conduct was less traditional than that of other ceremonial leaders.* (Emphasis added)[30]

The problem with extending this suggestive view too far is that it is difficult to find evidence that specific berdaches were involved in particular instances of religious change. Given the evidence, however, it is not unreasonable to suppose that such persons were involved in the initiation of social and religious change in the village societies.

These structural factors enabled and legitimated certain kinds of social change, but they do not provide a complete view of how changes in Mandan and Hidatsa religious traditions and practices occurred or what they meant in the experience of the people. Central to such an explanation were the creative capacities of the people who endured the pressures of disease, warfare, and frustration as their activities and life possibilities were increasingly limited. Among the Mandans and Hidatsas, creative interpretations accompanied both the development of ritual similarities and the maintenance of significant differences in the religious practices that surrounded hunting and agriculture.[31] Individuals and interpreting groups linked new forms of religious traditions and practices to those that already existed, forming a new cultural synthesis. Even though to the observer many religious practices looked the same, they were often linked to very different oral traditions. In this manner, Mandans and Hidatsas maintained a sense of continuity in the midst of social and religious change.

Animal calling rituals and rituals performed to insure the fertility and renewal of the buffalo provide instances of this sort of social change. Mandans and Hidatsas developed such rituals, and although they came to exhibit similarities at the level of performance, they were grounded in distinctive traditions. For this reason, the meaning of these activities was experienced differently within each group, and as the two peoples came into closer physical and cultural contact, these experienced differences remained. An examination of these rituals and the oral traditions that informed them will illustrate how rituals that look the same could have been experienced so differently.

As one example, the Buffalo Dance of the Okipa was grounded in complex traditions that recalled the time when all living things were imprisoned in Dog Den Butte by Hoita, the speckled eagle. The Okipa animal rituals were symbolic enactments that recalled the freeing of the animals and the end of the starvation of the people.[32] Among the Hidatsa and Awaxawi divisions, a very similar group of rituals for calling buffaloes rested on a quite different tradition concerning a marginalized young man, an Assiniboine boy named Raven Necklace, who had been taken prisoner by the Hidatsas.[33] This tradition drew clear symbolic boundaries between otherwise similar Mandan and Hidatsa rituals.

In a pattern typical of such narratives, Raven Necklace had an important experience that was evoked by an encounter with a powerful and important being. As Raven Necklace was about to push over a dead tree, this seemingly insignificant act caused him to hear a strange voice. "Raven Necklace," the voice said, "leave that tree alone, for it is my home. I have my young ones here and I do not want my home destroyed."[34] The voice belonged to a large owl who was the leader of the buffaloes whose spirits lived in various buttes in the surrounding territory. These buffalo spirits met periodically to perform rituals under the leadership of Owl, and because Raven Necklace did not destroy the creature's young, Owl transferred to him—and through him to the Hidatsas—the knowledge and ritual processes necessary to call buffaloes.

This power was made effective through the ritual of the Earthnaming bundle, which contained a buffalo skull and the head, wings, and claws of a speckled owl.[35] The owner of this bundle was accorded high status in Hidatsa society because he had the responsibility for enacting rituals that related the people to an essential food supply. This bundle was traditionally inherited from father to son, and because the knowledge surrounding the bundle and the accompanying ritual were quite complex, the training of a son or sons began at a very early age.

All three divisions of the Hidatsas had additional animal rituals, some of which they came to share with the Mandans.[36] There was one buffalo ritual among the Hidatsas, however, that was not shared by the Mandans. It is especially interesting because it is suggestive for understanding how some of the core symbols in these rituals often functioned.

This ritual, called Imitating Buffalo, arose as a consequence of the activities of a male figure called Blood Clot Man and a female figure called Buffalo Woman.[37] It also included references to First Creator and Lone Man, which indicates that processes of reinterpretation had been at work to incorporate some Mandan origin motifs. Blood Clot Man and Buffalo Woman were represented as being present at the beginning, when First Creator and Lone Man discovered Male Buffalo on the earth. Buffalo Woman was created by Village Old Woman when she provided females of each species to dwell upon the land with the males. In time, Buffalo Woman became transformed into a Hidatsa female, and this person came to play an important role in the Imitating Buffalo ritual.

The figure of a "bloody man" suggests some of the meanings evoked by the ritual.[38] On one level, the ritual involved the use of such objects as a buffalo hide and a buffalo skull. Human imitation of the buffalo in the ritual was believed actually to produce the conditions that were essential for the acquisition of animals in the hunt. On another level, participants reenacted the identities of the founders, the oral tradition becoming a text that shaped the ritual process. In this manner, certain important cognitive levels of the narrative were reproduced periodically in the experience of the group, which in turn strengthened the shared memorial tradition. On a deeper level, the gross actuality of a bloody hunt was connected through the ritual to the emotional level of the people's experience. Buffaloes were killed, actual blood was shed, and yet this primal, bloody reality was transmuted into a structure of meaning that transformed gross physicality into legitimate and appropriate activities: the acquisition, preparation, and consumption of food.

Another buffalo-calling ritual, the Painted Red Stick, was enacted in a similar manner by both the Mandans and the Hidatsas, but it was informed by very different origin narratives.[39] This ritual is interesting because it contained complex symbols and involved acts that are open to conflicting interpretations. It may be that the Red Stick ritual was adopted by the Hidatsas after their arrival on the Missouri River.[40] The Awatixas, who were the oldest residents on the river and the group with the longest associations with the Mandans, did not claim this ritual as a part of their tradition, although they did participate in it.[41]

The Mandan tradition does have a central core based on the activities of a figure named Corn Silk, a young woman who brought a strange little girl to the Mandan village.[42] The little girl in this narrative turned out to be a cannibal who proceeded to kill and eat the people. A typical response to this crisis occurred: A young man pledged to fast and consult the spirit world, since no one knew that the little girl was responsible for the situation. In the young man's vision, twelve buffalo bulls appeared. Each bull carried a red stick to which was attached buffalo hoofs, lungs, heart, and windpipe. The buffalo bulls revealed to the young man through a song that the people's problem was due to the cannibalistic activities of the little girl, who was known as Pretty Young Woman. Once the people learned of this, they burned the little girl, and as she burned, the people she had eaten were freed from her body. The tradition ended with the establishment of a bundle that included a buffalo robe and twelve red sticks.[43]

Hidatsa traditions had as their central characters buffalo bulls who were sometimes painted red and who carried red sticks. An Awaxawi tradition also included the figures of Buffalo, Sun, and Moon in the narrative.[44] This complex tradition cast Sun in a typically negative role as one who was threatening the Hidatsa villages with destruction. Buffalo Woman discerned that an ugly stranger who was winning all of the village goods through successful gambling was, in actuality, Sun. She devised a plan to defeat Sun. This plan required inviting all of the gods and spirits of the universe, including Sun, to a ritual during which the young men of the villages would give their wives to the spirits. Through a sexual encounter between the spirits and the human women, power might be transferred to the Hidatsas.

During the first three nights of the ritual, Sun refused to come closer than the edge of the village. Then on the fourth night Sun entered the village and, along with Moon, made his way to the lodge where the ritual was being held. Immediately upon his entry into the lodge, Buffalo Woman said to Sun: "I am your granddaughter. Why didn't you come before, you are the greatest god. We will go outside [for sexual intercourse], for you are my grandfather."[45] Sun tried to refuse contact with Buffalo Woman, but finally he could not sustain his resistance because, as the tradition explains, "Males have less will power than females in sexual matters."[46]

As a consequence of this sexual encounter, Sun lost his powers to Buffalo Woman. Subsequently, Buffalo Woman transferred the powers to the Hidatsas through the initiation of the Red Stick ritual. As was the case for the Mandans, the ritual involved a bundle, although the Hidatsa enactment was supervised by the owner of the Earthnaming bundle. Also, in this rendition Sun's power was transferred to the humans through the agency of an animal, while in other contexts buffaloes seemed to possess powers of their own that were transferred to the people.

Even though the Mandan and Hidatsa origin narratives differed, the ritual was similar at the performance level. A basic similarity lies in the act of sexual intercourse, which is present in all of the ritual enactments.[47] In addition, a core of shared meaning that developed among the two groups was visible in the pattern of beliefs that held that older, experienced hunters were successful because they had acquired special powers either from the buffaloes themselves or from other spirits. One way these powers could successfully be transferred to the younger generation was by the act of sexual

intercourse, which passed the older men's powers on to the younger hunters and their families. The Red Stick ritual was often initiated by a group
of younger men of the same age group. They approached the men in an
older age group, and if they reached an agreement with them, the ritual was
enacted.

The symbolism of the ritual related the people, through sexual acts, to
the buffaloes themselves. If the red sticks are interpreted as suggesting the
form and color of a male buffalo's sexual organ, then an otherwise murky
dimension of the Mandan ritual becomes clearer. Part of the ritual involved
the young wives, who were naked except for a buffalo robe, squatting down
on their heels and walking astraddle the red sticks that had been placed in
a line on the floor of the lodge.[48] This graphic representation of intercourse
with the buffaloes preceded intercourse with older hunters who possessed
buffalo power and who, through the ritual, became the animals who mediated power to the people.

Even though it is clear that sexual transfers of power were widespread in
Mandan and Hidatsa society and that these activities were probably viewed
by most as essential to the flourishing of the people, certain questions concerning the place of women in these rituals remain. For example, did women
in any sense consent to this activity? Did they believe that their role was
not only essential but also powerful? Or did the ritual actually mask what
can be understood to be clear examples of male exploitation of women in
these societies?

Some descriptions suggest that the Red Stick ritual, as well as other
rituals that involved sexual transfers of power, were not as disruptive for
women who had been married for some time and who had been prepared by
older females for their role. This point was illustrated by the experience of
Wolf Chief when he participated in the Red Stick ritual.[49] Wolf Chief had
a very young wife, and he was unsure, given her inexperience, how to broach
the matter of her participation. Wolf Chief's mother and the mother of the
young woman talked to each other and agreed that it would be a good thing
for the wife to do. Then the older women talked to the young wife, who
subsequently participated in the ritual and had intercourse with Walking
Chief, an older man who belonged to the clan of Wolf Chief's father. This
experience was so distressing to the young woman that she ran away and

hid herself for the remainder of the ritual. This forced Wolf Chief to take the wife of a clansman to participate with him on the remaining two nights of the ritual. It seems clear from this example that Wolf Chief's young wife did not fully consent to participate even though she did respond at some level to the encouragement of the older women.

As Mandan and Hidatsa contact with Europeans increased, there is stronger evidence for the exploitation of Indian women in such rituals. Europeans were perceived through traditional cultural categories as possessing astounding wealth, knowledge, and power. It did not take long for traders to learn how to gain access to the wives of younger men who were anxious to share in the traders' riches and power. From the Mandan and Hidatsa point of view, an appropriate ritual to achieve this purpose was one that involved a sexual encounter. The European point of view, being quite different, led to the increased exploitation of Mandan and Hidatsa women.

European men were not the only ones at fault, however. There is evidence that older Hidatsa men who had become marginal to the social and ritual life of the group might get together and make an offer of good luck to a younger man in exchange for the sexual services of his wife. This was clearly a corruption of the general practice, and it was interpreted as such by some Mandans and Hidatsas. Even though the offers of such men were often refused, some younger men did respond, probably because there were so many examples in the oral traditions of power transfers occurring through the agency of older men. Nevertheless, the corruption of the cultural pattern increased the possibility for the sexual exploitation of women within Mandan and Hidatsa society.[50]

The description of buffalo calling rituals would be incomplete without a discussion of the White Buffalo Cow society. This society was an age-graded women's organization that probably originated with the Mandans but that was transferred to the Hidatsas early in the nineteenth century.[51] This organization constituted an important locus of female power among Mandan and Hidatsa women, and it included the oldest women in the society. In contrast to previous descriptions of a creative reinterpretation of traditions and religious practices, both the ritual processes and the traditions of origin were virtually identical in Mandan and Hidatsa societies.

The shared origin narrative informed the Mandan and Hidatsa understanding of the White Buffalo Cow society's ritual.[52] This tradition opened with the portrayal of a man fasting outside his village during one of the coldest days of winter. This is a narrative projection of an actual historical practice that took place during periods in winter when animals became scarce and hunting was poor. On the fourth night, the faster heard a voice and had a vision. The figure in the vision was a man carrying two children. The strange man, who was actually Buffalo, instructed the faster to return to his village, prepare a feast of corn, and await the arrival of the winter buffaloes.

Soon after the faster returned to the village, a group of buffalo women arrived along with two buffalo children. The women instructed the people in the dance of the White Buffalo Cow society. When the buffalo women left the village, they left the two buffalo children behind. One buffalo child escaped and joined his mother, but the other remained in the village and became an Indian. Each year in the dead of winter, the White Buffalo Cow society would dance, and since one of the dancers symbolically became the buffalo child who had remained in the village, the winter herds were drawn near the village to see their kin.

White Buffalo Cow society transfer processes followed a standard pattern: If members of the White Buffalo group had held their positions for about ten years and if their numbers had been reduced by illness or death, younger women would negotiate the terms of the transfer with the older women. Each older woman would select as many as four "daughters" from among the younger women and would begin to prepare for them (or her) the requisite clothing and ritual objects to be used in the society's winter dances. The transfer involved not only clothing and objects but also instruction in the knowledge necessary for a proper performance of the ritual.[53] In the enactment of the ritual, participants included people who became, at the symbolic level, summer buffalo and the buffalo child described in the tradition of origin.[54]

The White Buffalo Cow society illustrates interesting gender characteristics that appear in the attitudes and practices that mature women shared. In the case of the lower (younger) women's societies, as well as in all men's societies, the transfer of membership required that a person give up all participatory rights in the society that he or she was leaving. This was not true for the White Buffalo Cow society, however. Older women who transferred out of this society did not lose all of their rights to continued participation in the rituals and activities of the group.[55]

The question of whether this feature was a function of gender differences, such as inclusiveness and diminished competitiveness among females as compared with males, cannot finally be settled. Perhaps the explanation lies in an attempt by the women to redress power imbalances produced by the strains placed on their societies due to increased European contact. This explanation is plausible, given the higher status that accrued to men as a consequence of increased participation in warfare. Whatever the underlying reasons, the result was the formation of an inclusive and powerful community of women in both the Mandan and Hidatsa societies. These societies created bonds among women that cut across other social structures and provided a context for female power and status to be maintained and reproduced through generational time.[56]

Whereas the symbolism of the Red Stick ritual projected a sexual relationship between male buffaloes and Mandan and Hidatsa women that was reinforced by an actual sexual encounter between young married women and older men, the White Buffalo Cow society projected a relationship between female buffaloes, human females, and a buffalo child who took on human form. In both cases, ritual processes and origin narratives established special affection and kinship relationships between the humans and the buffaloes. The differences in symbolic meaning were striking: In the buffalo-calling rituals, male-female imagery was grounded in sexual and reproductive symbolism, while in the White Buffalo Cow society origin account, female-female imagery was grounded in nurturance and childhood symbolism.

In addition, the White Buffalo Cow society evoked meanings surrounding blood that paralleled the blood imagery connected with the traditions that informed the Imitating Buffalo and Buffalo Corral rituals. Only women past menopause could become members of the White Buffalo Cow society. This rule was based on the belief that menstrual flows would drive the buffaloes away. This belief may have as much to do with the symbolic associations between blood and the actual death of animals—which might bring offense to the buffaloes—as it did with a more negative view of women, which has often been suggested by interpretations of such narratives.[57]

As was true for hunting, the levels of knowledge and concrete practices concerning agriculture were widely shared among the Mandans and Hidatsas. Agricultural rituals in these societies revolved around the figure of the Old Woman Who Never Dies. These traditions became very widely distributed, and the bundles that embodied their meaning were present in every Mandan and Hidatsa village.[58] These bundles were divided into primary bundles, which had direct connections with the Old Woman Who Never Dies, and secondary bundles, which shared in specific ways in the power of the primary bundle. By the nineteenth century, primary bundles were usually owned by males, which indicates probable changes in the relationship between gender, bundle ownership, and social status. Secondary bundle ownership was very widespread among women, and among the Mandans there were interesting differences in the way transfers of these bundles were understood. These differences rested on whether the transfer was initiated by a male or a female: "When a man bought [a bundle], his wives, sisters and brothers could purchase jointly. However, when a woman initiated the purchase, her sisters, brothers and their wives could purchase jointly, but the husband could not participate in the transfer or hold rights in the bundle."[59]

Even though the figure of the Old Woman Who Never Dies was present in the cultural inventory of both groups, the accounts concerning her activities were embedded in distinct traditions that drew symbolic boundaries between them. The major symbolic boundaries were created by the Mandans' incorporation of this female goddess within the Good Furred Robe narrative, while the Hidatsas integrated her into the Sacred Arrows narrative. Among the Mandans, she was incorporated into the corn bundles and their rituals as well. For example, a number of objects in the Mandan Robe bundle, such as the heads of water birds and a deer skull, were understood by the people to be related to this Old Woman.[60] For the Hidatsas, the Old Woman and her rituals appeared in the Sacred Arrow account after Two Men had instructed Unknown Man in the details of the Naxpike.[61] Despite the connections with major traditions that distinguished the two groups, the core elements of the Old Woman Who Never Dies narrative, as well as secondary bundles associated with this tradition, were shared, and everyday garden rituals tended to be almost identical. In the origin traditions, the Old Woman Who Never Dies was portrayed as a female being who possessed extraordinary fecundity as well as the secret of an inexhaustible supply of food. In the Mandan tradition, these complex meanings were evoked in the image of the Old Woman feeding two young men—a group of people in the Hidatsa rendition—from pots containing corn mush. No matter how much food they consumed, the pots were always replenished with an abundance of mush.[62] This image was connected with a broader symbolic network that evoked both a sense of dependence on the plant world for food and a belief that this world was usually generous to the people.

Both Mandan and Hidatsa traditions included descriptions of the relation of this Old Woman to the Corn Spirits, who traveled with the water birds to their winter home in her lodge and returned to the people in the spring, migrating up the Missouri River with the birds.[63] The two groups also shared the belief that the Old Woman's husband was a great snake, and such imagery was often associated with water, the river systems, and a sense of place.[64] On the robe that was believed to have belonged to Good Furred Robe, there was a painted representation of the Missouri River in the form of a great snake. The Robe bundle itself was believed to have an effect on the weather, the coming of sufficient rain, and abundant crops.[65]

Complementing the Old Woman Who Never Dies tradition were complex symbols that connected sky beings with earth and water beings, and both Mandan and Hidatsa narratives featured scenes in which sky beings became involved with Indian women through marriage. One such tradition represents a discussion between Sun and Moon. Sun asked Moon what kind of woman he wanted to marry. Moon replied that he had his eye on a handsome young woman from one of the Corn-Sheller villages. Sun did not agree that the Mandan women were so beautiful, because, "They have only one eye with wrinkles all over their faces when they look at me." Instead, he expressed desire for a Toad Woman, saying, "When they look at me they have such pretty blue eyes."[66]

Sun ended up marrying a Toad Woman, while Moon married a Mandan woman. As a consequence of the marriage, Moon became the father of a son, but in time the young woman began to long for her own people. Even though she had been warned of the dangers, the young woman dug up a large turnip. Through the hole left in the sky country by its root, she and her son descended toward the earth on a rope that had been made for her by the mice. She was only able to reach treetop level, however, because the rope was too short. Moon looked down and was angered, seeing his young wife and his son suspended above the treetops. In a rage he dropped a large stone on his wife's head and killed her. The young son survived and dropped from the end of the rope into a garden belonging to the Old Woman Who Never Dies. This young boy, who was cared for by the Old Woman, became known as Grandson in the traditions. He was portrayed as living on the earth for some time but finally returning to the land of the sky people, taking the form of a star.[67] The meanings evoked by this complex symbolic structure portray a relationship between sky, earth, and water beings that involved both conflict and tension. Rituals that were enacted had the task of renewing and maintaining this essential set of relationships and repairing them when, for whatever reason, they went awry.

The Goose society, another important women's society shared by the Mandans and Hidatsas, engaged in dances that were essential to the maintenance of these relations and to the success of the crops.[68] The Old Woman Who Never Dies tradition shaped Mandan and Hidatsa experience so deeply that it was taken for granted that the corn spirits who went in the fall to the Old Woman's lodge with the water birds would return again with the birds' spring migration—if the appropriate rituals were performed. The dance of the Goose Women was considered necessary to continue this cycle of agricultural fertility. The society danced during the spring, when the plant spirits were believed to be returning to the people, and during the fall, when they were returning to the lodge of the Old Woman Who Never Dies. Special Goose society rituals were also enacted when the gardens were threatened by periods of drought or by pests such as grasshoppers.

In addition to a buffalo robe, dress, and moccasins, the members of this society wore a headband made of goose skin with the head attached. Each woman carried an ear of corn wrapped in white sage. The ritual objects and special dress were prepared by women who were transferring out of the society for their younger "daughters" who were purchasing membership. A woman might select as few as one or as many as four "daughters," to whom she taught the songs, dances, and cultural meanings that surrounded the ritual process. At the end of a period of preparation, the transfer was completed. As was true for the White Buffalo Cow society, women leaving the Goose society did not give up their relationship to the dances and rituals or their special relationship with the younger women.

Membership in the Goose society and the White Buffalo Cow society brought women into contact with nonhuman persons and powers. The ritual participation of women was essential to successful hunting, and the activities of the Goose society placed them in a close relationship with the other side of the dual economy, the gardens. Because these women were younger than those in the White Buffalo Cow society, their menstrual flows were symbolically connected with notions of fertility. The moisture of their blood was essential to the growth of the plant foods upon which the flourishing of the people depended, and even though male participation as singers and male bundle ownership were features of some of the social processes surrounding women's roles, both of these societies provided women with powerful and somewhat autonomous social roles supported by religious traditions and practices.

In addition to the structural features in Mandan and Hidatsa societies that were important for understanding religious and social change, the creative activity of interpretation was at the center of both the continuities and the internal changes in ritual practice and oral traditions. Viewed from within the society, the elaboration of oral traditions connected elements drawn from the wider social environment to known webs of meaning. Religious changes that resulted from such syntheses appeared to the Mandans and Hidatsas as continuous with their experience rather than as threatening to their respective identities. This expanded understanding places the importance of Indian agency and interpretation at the center of processes of religious change. Furthermore, the changes that did occur happened in such a way that the reality of the Mandans and Hidatsas special identity as peoples, which was based on their distinctive religious traditions, was not sacrificed but was maintained even in the face of enormous social and psychological pressure.

6 ▿ ▿ ▿ ▿ ▿

Religious Transformations on the Northern Plains

Understanding how religious worlds of meaning were constructed, maintained, and changed among the Mandans and Hidatsas evokes a complex vision of social continuity and innovation. The responses of Northern Plains villagers to the appearance of changes in their environment sometimes took the form of innovations in their social structure. These innovations arose out of an interpretive process that enabled them to maintain a sense of social continuity and equilibrium in spite of the significant social changes they were undergoing. This interpretation should not obscure the pervasive suffering that engulfed these peoples during periods of destructive conflict, food shortages, epidemic diseases, and cultural confusion introduced by encounters with Europeans. Rather this study has attempted to provide an account of how, in the midst of these often tragic factors, Northern Plains peoples maintained their social identities while engaging in innovation. I have argued that religious energies often motivated the processes of reinterpretation that contributed to both continuity and change.

The Northern Plains was also an arena for social changes that transcended the Mandans and Hidatsas. These changes were introduced into the environment over time and were stimulated by massive population shifts that brought migrating people from different backgrounds into the area.

While it is true that the people who became the Mandans and the Hidatsas had been migrants themselves, now other people moved into the Northern Plains and became tipi-dwelling, nomadic buffalo hunters.[1] In the course of their social development toward a life as mobile hunters, many of these groups transformed their religious traditions and practices, as well as their economic and social structures.

The experiences of the Crows and the Cheyennes illustrate the role that religion played in shaping new individual and social identities among the migrating peoples who ultimately became horse nomads.[2] Religion played an essential role in the social transformation of these peoples, and in the process, religious traditions and practices were themselves transformed. The focus of this chapter is on those religious traditions and practices that seem essential to the development of Crow and Cheyenne identity as distinctive peoples.[3]

The people who became the Crows had once been kinspersons of the Hidatsas, with both groups speaking dialects of the same language. Neither the date when the Crows separated from the Hidatsas nor the circumstances surrounding their early movements are entirely clear.[4] What is certain is that the Crows gradually left their village life behind and moved westward to become nomadic buffalo hunters. An important part of the Crow identity as hunters arose as a consequence of creative transformations of religious traditions and practices.

The religious universe that organized Crow experience contained traditions and practices that were clearly related to their previous Hidatsa kinspersons.[5] There were other traditions and practices that formed distinct symbolic boundaries that identified the Crows as a people who possessed a unique identity. These symbolic boundaries were drawn in the origin narratives and in rituals that were often constructed out of preexisting oral narratives. Through a process of creative reshaping, these religious traditions and practices became unique to the Crow people.

Crow origin traditions shared with some of the Hidatsa accounts the image of a creator who formed the world out of mud that diving birds brought to the surface of primal waters. These traditions established the fundamental distinctiveness of the Crow people by associating them not only with a particular creator figure but also with a powerful plant person—

Tobacco. The creator in these narratives was Sun, who was often accompanied by another figure, Old Man Coyote. In other versions, Old Man Coyote, also known as First Worker, was the central figure.

Medicine Crow's narrative portrayed Sun and Old Man Coyote walking on the newly created earth. During their travels they met a number of beings who had gained life by their own powers—Wolf, Coyote, Rock, and Tobacco. Tobacco was the most important of these self-generating persons for understanding Crow identity. When Sun and Old Man Coyote first met this person, he had the appearance of a star who was standing on the earth. But as they approached, Star Man transformed himself into a Tobacco plant. After their encounter with this powerful being, Sun made people (Crows) out of mud. When they were animated, Sun gave the tobacco plant to the people and said, "From now on all the people shall have this, take it in the spring and raise it. It is the stars above that have assumed this form, and they will take care of you. This is the Tobacco plant. Take care of it and it will be the means of your living."[6]

Other important star references in Crow traditions told of the Crows' separation from the Hidatsas. After they separated, an anonymous Crow man had a powerful dream. In response, the man set out on a journey in search of the gift promised in his vision. On the side of a mountain he saw a shining object, a star, which he carefully wrapped up and took back to the people. After he returned, the man planted the star (Tobacco). When the plants had matured, he harvested them, keeping some seeds for the following year. In language that recalled the creation tradition, this man said that because of the Tobacco plant the Crows would become a people.[7]

The Hidatsas' traditions that told of their separation from the Crows provided additional insight into the role that religious traditions played in the constitution of social identity. These traditions, as did those among the Crows, told of an argument that broke out among the people over the division of a buffalo. This social conflict led to the separation of Crow groups from the rest of the people. Among the Crow groups that left and moved west were seven singers who participated in a Tobacco ritual. These persons were responsible for singing the Tobacco songs, and they were probably related to an early ritual process that surrounded the Tobacco plant.[8]

Whether these narratives accurately represented historical events is less significant than the fact that an important ritual process developed among the Crows that was focused on tobacco. As they moved toward their life as nomadic buffalo hunters, they took with them a practice of gardening that was centered not on food production but on the cultivation, preservation, and renewal of their identity as a people.[9] A discussion of the Tobacco society will bring the symbolic materials on astral beings, plants, and their relation to the construction of social identity into clearer focus.

By the late nineteenth century, the Tobacco society had become a very complex organization. In its earlier forms the society may have contained as few as five divisions and was probably composed of people of mature age. Strikes Both Ways was almost a hundred years old when she told one interpreter that the Weasel, Otter, Elk, White Bird, and Tobacco chapters comprised the society.[10] Later the divisions multiplied until almost every adult in Crow society, both male and female, was a member. The association of the tobacco plant with the stars established a broad symbolic boundary between the Crows and their neighbors, including their former kinspersons, the Hidatsas. The ritual planting of tobacco each year was a primary activity that maintained and renewed these boundaries.

The divisions of the Tobacco society arose as a consequence of a dream or vision experience. Medicine Crow's experience was typical.[11] As a youth he went out to fast, and after having severed a finger joint as an offering to Sun, he had a powerful vision of a young man and a young woman who were each holding two hoops, one hung with feathers and the other made of strawberries. Both had a strawberry, a tobacco seed, and the body of a red-headed woodpecker tied at the back of their heads. They were tobacco plants, and they revealed to Medicine Crow their desire to join the tobacco plant with the strawberries. As a consequence of this vision, Medicine Crow founded the Strawberry division of the Tobacco society.

Dreams and visions had such deep social legitimation in Crow society that the expansion of the Tobacco society by this means was natural. Furthermore, there was widespread participation of both men and women in the activities of the society's divisions, as well in the seeking of visions. Rather than the division of roles and social power between males and females that arose between war/hunting and agriculture in the village societies, the Tobacco society was nonhierarchical and inclusive.[12] Both sexes participated together in rituals that maintained and renewed the identity of the entire people.

The growth in membership within the various divisions of the society was accomplished by means of an adoption ritual that included an exchange of property. The people who were adopted, usually a married man and woman, stood in a kinship relation to the person who was adopting. They were the children, and the adopting person was the parent. The ritual language that surrounded this part of the interaction was suffused with birth imagery. People chosen for membership in the Tobacco society were born into a new relationship; they became, with others, responsible for nurturing some of the symbols that were central to the construction of the Crow universe.

In earlier times, people usually made a pledge to join the society under conditions of illness or duress, which may account for its relatively small size during this period. Later, membership was expanded by means of adoption. Preceding the adoption process, a gift was given by the adopting "parent" to the persons invited into the society. If the persons were adopted, the giving of gifts would be reversed, and even greater wealth flowed toward the parent in return. The transfer of wealth still did not lead to sharp divisions of status and power between the more recent members and people who had longer tenure in the society. All were involved together in a ritual practice that did not allow such distinctions to take deep root.

After people had been approached for adoption, there followed a time of preparation during which the individuals learned Tobacco songs and participated in a number of the dances held by the particular division they were joining. After the time of preparation was over, initiation into the division was performed in a lodge specially constructed for this purpose. The lodge was made of cottonwood poles joined at the top, forming the shape of a tipi. Part of the lodge was covered with branches and part with buffalo skins, but a space was left open on one side so that sunlight could enter. At the center of the lodge was a rectangular space constructed of willow arches and bounded on each side by logs of equal length. According to some Crow interpretations, this structure was revealed in the origin narrative of the Tobacco society, and Plenty Hawk told one interpreter that it represented the Tobacco garden itself.[13]

Further preparations for the adoption ritual took place in a separate tipi. The faces of both the men and the women were painted, the individuals who performed this task having received their privilege from a vision. After the members joined in a number of dances and some had unwrapped their medicine bundles, the procession to the adoption lodge began. Four stops were made along the way, and at each stop songs were sung. The procession was under the leadership of a woman who wore a headdress made of juniper leaves and carried a pipe to be placed on the altar that had been constructed in the adoption lodge.

The activities of the Tobacco society's divisions focused on the yearly planting of tobacco. The entire Crow society moved near the garden site, where the seeds were prepared by a man or woman known as a mixer. Then the members of the Tobacco society approached the garden, again stopping four times along the way. This procession was headed by a woman who held before her the skin of a water animal such as a beaver or an otter. The power of this animal would bring nourishing rain to the crop.

After the garden site was prepared and the seeds planted, a number of small sweat lodges, believed to be very powerful, were constructed. In addition, a large sweat lodge was built, and the members of the Tobacco society regularly purified themselves within this enclosure. All was now in readiness for the appearance of the plants and the renewal of social energy that accompanied their flourishing. When the plants were ready, they were harvested and the seeds were preserved for use during the next year.

While Crow religious practice included a Sun Dance, as well as a number of other ritual objects and processes, the Tobacco society was among the oldest of these forms.[14] If some Tobacco singers left with the bands that separated from the Hidatsas, sources of ritual knowledge and perhaps a religious organization existed at that time. The later form of the Tobacco society must have been the successor of this early religious organization. While the ritual planting and harvesting of tobacco may have been a part of the culture that the Crows shared with their earlier kinspersons, an equivalent of the Tobacco society did not develop among the Hidatsas.[15] The bands that separated from the Hidatsas apparently took an earlier form of the tobacco ritual with them and developed it into a complex source of their separate identity as a people.

In the Crow origin traditions, the Tobacco plant was a powerful astral person who granted the gift of himself to the people. At the symbolic level, this gift was experienced as formative for the identity of the people. The traditions and practices that portrayed this social identity were embodied in communities of memory that were formed of individuals, both men and women, who had extensive spiritual experiences mediated through dreams and visions. Knowledge of these traditions and practices became widespread among the people because at least the general outlines were transmitted through generational time rather than becoming esoteric lore dominated by a smaller shamanistic group.

The Crow identity was made secure because the Star Man who was Tobacco was also embodied in a ritual process and a social organization, the Tobacco society, which was expanded from time to time by the energy released through the visions of individuals. This expansion did not detract from its central function, however, which was to maintain and renew the symbolic boundaries that constituted the Crows as a people. As they acquired the forms of life associated with buffalo hunting, the social transformations that they endured were energized by root symbols that surrounded Tobacco. Additional religious traditions and practices, such as the Sun Dance, contributed to the establishment of these cultural boundaries, but the Tobacco society seems to have been the essential feature that stood at the beginning of the differentiation of the Crows from the Hidatsas and their movement toward becoming a distinct people.

The Cheyenne experience provides an interesting comparative case. At least some of the people who were to become the Cheyennes lived for a time in or near the villages of the Mandans and the Hidatsas. At this point in their history, they built earth lodges and practiced subsistence agriculture in addition to hunting buffalo and small game. They may have taken fish from the Missouri River and its tributaries just as their village neighbors did. Even though these people spoke an Algonquian dialect while the Mandans and Hidatsas spoke Siouan dialects, they lived productively on the Missouri River before moving on to become fully nomadic buffalo hunters living in skin tipis. Their transformation into Plains hunters may have involved a creative appropriation and reinterpretation of particular religious traditions that led to the emergence of new religious traditions.

A discussion of Cheyenne migrations will provide a wider context for understanding their interaction with the Missouri River peoples. Although many of the details remain in contention, it is fairly clear that in the latter part of the seventeenth century Cheyenne groups lived near the headwaters of the Mississippi River in the vicinity of Lake Superior.[16] They probably lived in small villages, moved about in canoes, and subsisted on wild rice and small game. Sometime during the late seventeenth century, they were forced from their territory, probably as a consequence of pressures by the Assiniboines and Crees. The migration of groups of Cheyennes from their earlier homeland led some of them finally to the Missouri River. Depending on the dates one chooses to accept, the complex and uneven transition of these groups from an eastern woodlands context to a village context on the Missouri River and then to a mobile buffalo-hunting people probably spanned more than a century, perhaps from about 1680 to 1790.[17]

Rather than moving as a society, their westward migration was probably undertaken in small groups.[18] Some bands may have crossed the Missouri River much earlier than others, and some may have drifted farther west in the direction of the Black Hills to become pedestrian buffalo hunters until the arrival of the horse in the mid-eighteenth century. During the course of these migrations, the Cheyennes incorporated another Algonquian-speaking group, the Sutaios. According to tradition, the Cheyennes assimilated the Sutaio culture Hero, Erect Horns, and it was this figure who brought the Sun Dance to the people.[19]

It is not possible to differentiate Cheyenne village sites from those of the Mandans and Hidatsas, since their material cultures were so similar during this period. But evidence in Cheyenne and Sioux traditions, as well as the testimony of individuals, demonstrates that they built earth lodge villages on the Missouri, where they lived in much the same fashion as the older village societies. By the time of Lewis and Clark, these villages had been abandoned and the Cheyennes had become a buffalo-hunting people living in the vicinity of the Black Hills in South Dakota.[20]

The situation may have been even more complex. Some oral traditions claimed that some Cheyenne groups continued to garden after they moved to the Black Hills.[21] Thus the movement to full nomadism that was completed just before the time of Lewis and Clark was preceded by a period during which "some Cheyennes were nomadic hunters while others were sedentary horticulturalists—simultaneously."[22] Furthermore, some Cheyennes may have been farming on the Missouri River at the same time that others were farming and hunting in the vicinity of the Black Hills.

In the first chapter we encountered the tradition of interpretation that focused on cultural interchange between the village societies and peoples who were migrating into the Northern Plains. This argument held, among other things, that the emergence of important aspects of the cultures of the Plains nomads were the product of such cultural interaction. The Cheyenne groups who lived for a time near the Mandans and Hidatsas are of particular interest because they provide an opportunity not only to explore the implications of this earlier tradition but also to provide a clearer picture of the role that religion played in their cultural transformation.

Given these considerations, it is significant that the Cheyennes and the Awatixa division of the Hidatsas shared core elements of a culture hero tradition. At the center of each tradition were meanings evoked in rituals focused around sacred arrows. Although there was a general similarity between Cheyenne and Hidatsa traditions, each group understood its culture hero to have a distinctive identity. The hero's identity was appropriated by each group as a central ingredient in their own self-understanding, drawing a symbolic boundary that separated it from other groups. A more detailed comparison will illustrate these similarities and differences.

In the analysis of the Awatixa Charred Body origin narrative in chapter 3 we saw that the tradition centered on a culture hero who was an Arrow Person.[23] This figure descended from the sky country, defeated dangerous powers, and made the earth country safe for the migration of the sky clans. These people established thirteen villages along the Missouri River, becoming at the symbolic level the predecessors who established the Hidatsa village and clan structure.

In the course of his career, Charred Body killed an earth Indian, the daughter of a chief who refused his marriage proposal, setting the stage for a conflict between the earth and sky peoples. Even though this conflict was protracted, Charred Body's sister survived, only to be killed by a monster, Man With No Head. The twins she was carrying, Lodge Boy and Spring Boy, survived this attack. When they matured, they became Two Men, who possessed the arrow power of Charred Body. They resolved the conflict between the earth and sky peoples by defeating Long Arm, the chief of the sky people. As a token of reconciliation, Long Arm transferred the Naxpike to Two Men, and they in turn transferred the ritual to the people through their son, Unknown Man. An elaboration of the Cheyenne tradition will illustrate both the similarities and the differences between Charred Body and the Cheyenne culture hero.[24]

The Cheyenne tradition shared a fundamental structural feature with the Awatixa narrative: both traditions associated their culture heroes with sacred arrows.[25] The Cheyenne narrative centered on a culture hero named Sweet Medicine. Most versions of this tradition opened with the birth of a baby who exhibited special powers when he was very young.[26] One version said that "He surprised the people by knowing so much."[27] As a youth, Sweet Medicine revealed his power by decapitating himself in the company of leading Cheyenne shamans. Then he rejoined his head to his body, demonstrating for all to see that he had unique status among the people. Later, as a young man, he came into conflict with a Cheyenne chief over a black buffalo. Sweet Medicine had killed the animal and was taking the robe, which the chief wanted for himself. In the altercation over the robe, Sweet Medicine killed the chief (recall that Charred Body killed a chief's daughter). After killing the chief, Sweet Medicine became a fugitive from Cheyenne society. He was continually pursued, but in each encounter Sweet Medicine managed to escape, often by assuming the form of a bird or animal.

These descriptions of encounters between Sweet Medicine and the people were embedded in a migration narrative that spanned an indefinite period during which the Cheyennes were said to have moved great distances. After a series of events in which Sweet Medicine was betrayed by his family (especially his brother), the Cheyennes found themselves without food and were facing starvation. At this point the tradition relates how the culture hero transformed the inside bark of an elm tree into buffalo meat, and snow into marrow fat. He provided four Cheyenne boys with this food and told them to take it to the starving people. The people ate their fill, yet there was still meat and marrow fat left over.[28]

After feeding the people, Sweet Medicine returned to the camp, married a chief's daughter, and performed a four-day buffalo ritual, at the end of which a great communal kill was made. Four years after the successful re-introduction of the game to the Cheyenne environment, Sweet Medicine and his wife (some versions say a young woman who later became his wife) left the people, bound for a destination in the Black Hills identified by the Cheyennes as Bear Butte. Upon entering the butte through a stone door, they saw first a coyote skin and then four hawk-feathered arrows pointing in the same direction. After that they encountered four eagle-feathered arrows. The butte was filled with mysterious, powerful persons, one of whom asked Sweet Medicine which arrows he preferred. The culture hero expressed interest in the eagle-feathered arrows.

Sweet Medicine and his wife were instructed in the use of the arrows, which were to be kept in a coyote-skin quiver and wrapped in the hide of a ritually killed buffalo. The culture hero's wife, who was painted red, was also instructed in the care of the arrows and their proper mode of transportation. This instruction was said to have lasted for four years, at the end of which time Sweet Medicine and his wife emerged from the butte, returned to the people, and instructed them in the ritual of the arrows.[29]

The ritual process developed along the familiar pattern: It arose in response to the vow of an individual and it took four days to complete. On the first day the people formed an encampment that resembled a new-moon crescent, and the pledger erected his tipi. The people brought the pledger items that symbolized their desire to be related to the transcendent powers associated with the Sacred Arrow bundle. On the second day, they erected a large conical tipi. This was the Medicine Arrow Lodge, and it evoked memories of Sweet Medicine and of Bear Butte, where he received the arrows. On the third day, Cheyenne ritual leaders prepared sticks, each of which represented a family group. These sticks were passed through a cleansing smoke, an act believed to be efficacious for each family. On the fourth day the Sacred Arrows were renewed and their wrappings and feathers repaired. In the afternoon they were placed on a pole. Two of the arrows pointed toward the sky and two toward the earth.

Unlike many other bundles on the Northern Plains, the Sacred Arrow bundle was not transferred but rather was cared for by a religiously and ritually qualified keeper. This man's body was scarified, and four strips of flesh were removed from various areas on his body, powerfully evoking the transcendent powers of the four directions. On his chest a circle of flesh symbolizing the sun was removed, and directly above this sun his flesh was cut so as to form a crescent shape—a moon symbol. The keeper of the Arrow bundle bore on his body the symbols that reminded the people of their special relationship to the powers that met Sweet Medicine in the sacred mountain.

Central to the arrow ritual was what could be called the moral renewal of the group. Through the physical restoration and repair of the parts of the arrows, moral conflicts like murder were resolved and the Cheyenne social world was renewed. Also important were the powers that the arrows had to insure an adequate supply of food and protection against enemies. Two of the arrows were viewed as especially powerful in war, and two were essential for a successful hunt. The reception of this powerful Arrow bundle was fundamental to the Cheyenne movement toward their identity as nomadic buffalo hunters.[30]

In both the Hidatsa and the Cheyenne traditions, the culture heroes came into conflict with their respective peoples in similar ways. In both cases the arrows were powerful in hunting and war, and both groups evolved ritual processes that surrounded bundles associated with these objects. Further, the two traditions possessed a similar symbolic core that associated culture heroes with powerful arrows. On their way to becoming nomadic hunters, the Cheyennes may have creatively appropriated some of the elements of the Charred Body narrative in their construction of the Sweet Medicine tradition.[31] Further evidence is needed of possibilities for culture contact that may have led to the reimagination of Cheyenne religious traditions.

Cheyenne contact with Hidatsa arrow traditions could have occurred when groups of these people settled on the Missouri River, locating themselves between the Mandans on the north and the Arikaras on the south. In this case, the creative appropriation of Arrow symbolism may have led to the construction of a culture hero tradition and a new identity for the Cheyennes. Harold Ottaway has said that "Sometime between 1730 (when the Cheyenne bands began moving independently from the Sheyenne River to the Missouri) and 1795 (which marked the abandonment of the earthlodge village near Fort Yates) it appears the Awatixa introduced the Sacred Arrow 'complex' to the Cheyenne."[32]

A more recent analysis of the relationship between the Cheyennes and the Hidatsas has argued that they had been in contact in eastern North Dakota and western Minnesota for many generations before their respective migrations to the Missouri River.[33] This interpretation lends further support to the idea that the Cheyennes created central aspects of their identity as a consequence of the creative appropriation of arrow symbolism, but this view places the Cheyenne-Hidatsa interaction earlier. Whether the construction of traditions occurred on the Missouri River or before, the arrow traditions of both the Hidatsas and the Cheyennes have been linked together by contemporary Cheyenne religious leaders.[34]

The picture is made even more complex when we consider that the emergence of the Cheyennes as a people involved the integration of several bands into a single social and political unit. Two of the earliest bands have been identified as the Aortas and the Eaters. The two groups had separate origin traditions, and the Aortas were more closely associated with agriculture, while the Eaters were predominantly hunters. Although these two bands may have been related, they were constituted as a single people by the Sweet Medicine tradition.[35] After their formation as Sweet Medicine's people in the early 1700s, the Aortas and Eaters were joined by the Sutaios.[36]

While it is clear that some of the Cheyenne bands lived on the Missouri River for a time, the spread of arrow symbolism is difficult to trace directly. Cheyenne and Awaxawi traditions concerning their interactions before the smallpox epidemic of 1782 may provide additional evidence. As a consequence of a conflict with the Hidatsas proper, the Awaxawis had moved downstream and established a village, where they lived for a time near the Cheyennes who had villages around the Fort Yates region.[37] Since the Awaxawis arrived on the Missouri River after the Awatixas, they had assimilated from the early group a detailed knowledge of the Charred Body tradition. Not only did the Awaxawis know this tradition, they also shared a bundle and a ritual process that could easily have become known to the Cheyennes near Fort Yates.

The Awaxawi bundle was attributed to the Charred Body tradition, and the bundle itself contained two sacred arrows.[38] According to the Charred Body tradition, Unknown Man gave this arrow bundle, along with the Naxpike, to the Hidatsas. The ritual that was enacted focused on the figure of the grizzly bear in the Charred Body tradition. This animal was one of the helpers of Old Woman Who Never Dies, and in some versions of the tradition the arrows were painted red and black, recalling the color symbolism present in some versions of the Sweet Medicine tradition. Imagery related to success in hunting and warfare was associated with this bundle and its ritual, elements that were shared by the Cheyenne arrow ritual. Each time the bundle was transferred, the sacred arrows were central objects in the ritual process, and the participants in the ceremony included people who played the roles of Two Men and First Creator.

Bears Arm, who was born around 1850, was a hereditary owner of the principal Awaxawi Grizzly Bear bundle. He traced his patrilineal rights to this bundle through his father, Old Woman Crawling, and his great grandfather, Crow Bull. Ultimately, of course, he legitimated his rights through appeal to the Charred Body tradition.[39] If Bears Arm's great grandfather owned a Grizzly Bear bundle containing sacred arrows, then a version of this bundle and its ritual were part of the Hidatsa cultural symbolism and practice at the time when the Awaxawis lived near the Cheyennes in the vicinity of Fort Yates.

Since the Awaxawis were on friendly terms with the Cheyennes, it is plausible that some groups of Cheyennes heard portions of the Charred Body tradition and observed the ritual of the Grizzly Bear bundle. While it is not possible to provide more conclusive evidence, the circumstances are very suggestive, and such experiences might well have occurred. If the Cheyennes did observe the arrow ritual or heard portions of the Charred Body tradition, it is at least plausible to argue that they may have appropriated some of these symbolic elements to supplement their own bundle traditions and the associated practices. As the Cheyennes transformed themselves from village dwellers to mobile hunters, the bundle and its symbolic horizons could have been elaborated and linked to the figure of Sweet Medicine. Out of some such process of creative reinterpretation, the Cheyennes could have given rise to a new social and cultural identity.[40] Since the Grizzly Bear bundle and the sacred arrows were finally distributed among all three divisions of the Hidatsas, as well as among the Mandans, there were probably many opportunities for Cheyenne observation and appropriation.

Another, perhaps more influential, context for creative interaction between the Cheyennes and Hidatsa religious practices may have been the Naxpike ritual. This ritual centered on a bundle containing sacred arrows, and it is likely that Cheyennes living in or near Hidatsa villages would have observed this ceremony, and some of them may have participated in various levels of the ceremony. Such participation may have been another source for the creative appropriation of symbolic materials associated with powerful arrow beings. If the Sweet Medicine tradition was already in existence when such interactions occurred, it could still have been supplemented and expanded by these encounters. In addition to these examples, there were countless occasions when such creative interactions could have taken place.[41]

These materials formed an essential background for the construction of traditions that gave rise to the ritual of the sacred arrows among the Cheyennes. Whether Sweet Medicine was a historical person or a figure who came to exist through the medium of an oral tradition that became widely shared is not as important as the fact that this tradition contributed in an essential way to the emergence of the Cheyenne identity as a hunting people.[42] The place where the arrows were received by Sweet Medicine symbolized this new identity in a dramatic manner:

> Nowahwas, or Bear Butte, is located in southwestern South Dakota, near Sturgis. To the east are the Cheyenne River villages previously occupied by the Cheyennes. To the west are the Black Hills, where the Cheyennes wandered early in their nomadic days. And to the south are the Sand Hills of Nebraska, and the Republican and Smoky Hill drainage areas which have always been well-watered grazing territories, first for the buffalo and now for cattle. Bear Butte is ideally suited as a location for a prophecy of culture change—on the edge of the network of riverine horticulture sites, and overlooking the Great Plains proper.[43]

Given the previous evidence, the core symbolism of powerful arrows associated with a bundle that was given to the people by a culture hero may have arisen as a consequence of interactions with Hidatsa groups. This symbolism and the ritual processes that embodied it became, by means of the creative process of appropriation, thoroughly infused with meanings that were distinctively Cheyenne. For the Cheyennes, Sweet Medicine had a different identity from the Hidatsa figure of Charred Body. There was no confusion over this fact, just as there was no doubt that the special gifts of the power to conquer enemies and to be successful in hunting had been granted by Sweet Medicine to the Cheyennes. The Sweet Medicine tradition and the ritual of the Sacred Arrows became a central identity-forming institution among the Cheyennes; it was through this institution that the Cheyennes were able to transform themselves into a fully nomadic people.[44]

Clearly, religious traditions and ritual processes were central to the social transformations of both the Crows and the Cheyennes. But religious traditions and ritual processes functioned in complex ways in these societies. At one level, they unified experience and provided the people with a coherent world order. In this role, religious energies were conservative in nature, shaping individual memory and group tradition in a manner that produced a sense of continuity and identity. But at another level, religious traditions and ritual processes were also innovative. They energized human responses to events in their worlds that threatened to dislocate cultural meanings and to render their past traditions and identities problematic. Under such conditions, Northern Plains peoples responded by generating new traditions or new interpretations of old traditions, or by creatively appropriating the traditions of others. All three of these processes characterized the responses of the groups that have been studied.

As the groups of indigenous people in North America who were to become Plains Indians began to respond to the pressures generated by Europeans and other Indian peoples, their sense of shared meanings concerning identity and destiny were sometimes subjected to dislocation. Clearly the people who became the Cheyennes experienced dislocations in the meaning structure of their social world as they were dislodged from their previous homelands and began their migrations to the Northern Plains. And even though the Crows had memories of their previous existence as gardeners, they underwent significant social transformations as well.[45]

The Cheyennes represent an example of a people who, in the course of their migration to the Northern Plains, created new cultural forms and expanded pre-existing cultural traditions. In this culture-creating activity they may have appropriated elements, such as arrow symbolism and perhaps a bundle, that were already in existence in the social environment of the Missouri River. By reinterpreting and reconstructing symbolic meanings and their embodiment in ritual processes that mediated a new sense of identity and destiny, the Cheyennes generated, through their religious symbolism and ritual processes, a set of social changes that allowed them to make the transition to a hunting economy. As the ritual process associated with Tobacco had transformed the Crows, the arrow ritual associated with Sweet Medicine was a creative innovation that led to the formation of what became Cheyenne culture on the Northern Plains.

7 ▽ ▽ ▽ ▽ ▽

American Indian Religions and the Construction of Cultures

In the previous chapters, religion is understood as a symbolic reality embodied in oral traditions and enacted in ritual processes. Religious traditions and practices brought humans into contact with beings that transcended the everyday world. These transcendent beings were believed to have given rise both to humans and to their particular experienced world, including some but not usually all of its life forms. These beings engendered in the people a sense of special identity, setting them apart from others in their environment. Religion was also interpreted as occupying a central role in the way Native Americans understood social change within their societies. When a crisis or a new situation appeared, symbolic systems and ritual processes were changed through the activity of creative interpreters and interpreting groups.

Religious traditions provided a rich narrative structure that gave concrete shape to Native American social worlds. As is the case with human social worlds in general, Native Americans experienced relations with contemporaries, predecessors, and successors. Relations with contemporaries were structured in the context of a shared world of everyday experience. Oral traditions evoked powerful memories of predecessors, and these memories were periodically revitalized in rituals. Native Americans projected a vision of successors in their desire for children and grandchildren, the people who would carry on their names and traditions.

A sense of difference came from the content produced by and mediated through traditions that were specific to each society. The oral traditions spoke about human others, such as famous leaders and other ancestors, some of whom were important but unknown. Beyond the human, there were worlds populated by animal and plant beings, as well as persons such as Thunder, the Four Directions, and a wide variety of powerful others. Though they transcended the everyday world, these persons were often related to the people through kinship, and they were clearly sources of the power that was essential for humans to flourish.

The meanings evoked by particular oral traditions formed the culture-specific content of what was experienced as the natural and social worlds. Each of these experiences of the meaning of others, human and nonhuman (society and nature), did have a certain typicality among groups of people who shared the same general environment. But looked at from within, each group developed specialized sensibilities concerning the meaning of non-human others—such as plants, animals, birds, and fish—as well as the other features of their world, such as the mountains and river systems. The predecessors, both human and more than human, who were important for constituting social identity and for maintaining life, were likewise named and understood in ways that were distinctive for each group.

Native American religious traditions, as well as the ritual processes that preserved and mediated their meanings, were central to the construction of these societies in ways that were similar to but also different from contemporary state-based societies. In the latter, group identity is constructed on the basis of shared traditions and is mediated in the public rituals of the civil religion. There are monuments, holidays, special predecessors, and group emblems, such as flags, and these elements are embodied in public rituals that rehearse and mediate, more or less successfully, a sense of group identity and destiny.[1] Often these symbols and rituals of civil religion seem most powerful during times of external or internal crisis. State-based societies also seek to maintain their symbolic boundaries by defining their members (citizens versus noncitizens) and through public education that transmits knowledge of the central traditions of the group to each new generation.

These features are functionally similar to some of the social processes that were found in Native American societies on the Northern Plains. These societies sought to preserve their social identities by devising ways of maintaining their cultural boundaries. Predecessors that were important to the society were celebrated in periodic ritual processes, and specific groups acquired status on the basis of their knowledge of these traditions. Informal but powerful processes of socialization prepared children to enter fully into the linguistic and cultural landscape and to assume an identity as members of a specific people.

But symbolic boundaries were maintained by social processes that were different from those in state-based societies. One critical difference was the way the symbolic meanings that formed social identity were mediated. In large state-based societies, meanings are carried not only in oral traditions associated with founding predecessors but also in documents, such as constitutions, and in laws that are ultimately backed by force. Despite the fact that they are embodied in writing, these meanings are not immune to reinterpretation. Social change arises out of periods characterized by conflicts of interpretation that may issue in a new social vision, as well as new or reformed social institutions and practices.

Almost all social knowledge, including religious traditions and rituals, that informed Northern Plains societies and that shaped their identities was carried orally. While rich symbols were often emblazoned in human flesh and on the skins of tipis, and while dense meanings were carried by the entities enfolded in bundles, the worlds of Northern Plains peoples were formed and reformed through the system of signs and symbols mediated by particular languages. The fact of pervasive orality adds what seems to be a precarious feature of these societies compared with societies based on writing. They were precarious in the sense that cultural identity and the maintenance of symbolic boundaries depended on continuities of social interaction that supported the rehearsal of oral traditions and that fostered their ritual transmission across social time. If the bearers died without transmitting the tradition, all or part of this level of cultural knowledge and practice would be lost, and irretrievably so.[2]

Despite this apparent fragility, and even in the face of what otherwise would seem to be overwhelming events, such as genocide and the devastating impact of epidemic diseases, Northern Plains societies maintained and transformed their traditions. Important cultural meanings embodied in living bundles and their accompanying ritual processes continued to be transmitted to people who sought to maintain their relationship to important powers and beings who transcended the human. Even in the most desperate of circumstances, elements of the oral culture and cultural objects were transmitted and preserved, providing a barrier against the total loss of social identity.

The preservation of social identity was made possible through powerful communities of memory and interpretation. These tenacious communities had the capacity to reinterpret and project new understandings of their experience, as well as to preserve elements that were vital to social identity. In these groups there was a constructive relationship between memory, interpretation, and religious traditions. The Mandans and the Hidatsas, as well as the people who became the Cheyennes and the Crows, were characterized by this constructive relationship. Religious traditions and practices were at the center of the social construction and reconstruction of their identities, and the social changes that arose as a response to innovations in their environments depended on religiously grounded processes of reinterpretation.

When the historical context of Northern Plains religions is understood from this perspective, we can identify additional characteristics, some of which may be found among the religions of other Native Americans as well. A discussion of these characteristics may not only aid us in understanding aspects of the Native American religious past but may also shed light on the present situation.

First, the religious traditions that were central to Mandan, Hidatsa, Cheyenne, and Crow rituals had experiential reality when the peoples established productive relations with the powers that were believed to have granted them their existence as separate societies. When such relations were properly established, hunting was bountiful, agriculture was fruitful, enemies were kept at bay, and life was good. In short, relations with transcendent others were judged appropriate when the rituals produced *results* in the everyday world. Hunting, agriculture, and warfare were clearly activities that required human skill and organized knowledge to produce results, but these results would not be forthcoming without the infusion of power mediated in the religious traditions and enacted in ritual within each of the societies.[3]

In Northern Plains societies, the religious quest focused on acquiring sufficient power to preserve identity, foster life, and provide protection for individuals and the group. Rather than being *true* with respect to other religious perspectives, the people expected their religious traditions and rituals to be *effective*. The efficaciousness of traditions and rituals was revealed in the consequences that flowed from their enactment. If they were effective, humans would be nourished by a plentiful food supply, and their social existence would not only receive protection but would flourish.[4]

As different cultural groups came into increasing interaction with each other on the Northern Plains, they desired to guard against the loss of individual and group power. At the same time, they were mutually curious, and often sought to acquire the power released by the religious entities and actions of other individuals and groups. If the traditions and rituals of one group seemed more efficacious, another group might attempt to reproduce this power. Such impulses often led to formal transfers of traditions, bundles, songs, and dances between groups. Traditions and rituals such as those associated with the Okipa and the Naxpike were not transferred, however, because they were associated with core symbols that defined the group as a people.

Second, even though transfer processes and the imitative reproduction of certain rituals and symbolic objects took place on the Northern Plains, there was nothing in these religions like the missionary impulse that characterized European Christianity. One of the deep and tragic conflicts between Native American religions and various Christian groups and their missionaries lay in the fact that Christian missionaries claimed that their religious views were true in a way that rendered Native American religious experiences, traditions, and practices false or even perverted. These conflicts deepened when missionary activities became associated with the attempt to conquer and subordinate Native American peoples.[5]

Even though there were religious interchanges among groups, Native American peoples were not motivated to convert others, because they did not believe that one religion was true while the other was less true or even false. Evangelism and conversion were not the point of these religions.[6] Indeed, to offer the power of one's central religious rituals to another was viewed as dangerous since such activity might cause a diminished relation of one's group to life-giving powers. To repeat the point made above, people carefully guarded the meanings that were mediated in their religious universes and that were deeply connected with personal or social identity, with the continuity of their lives, and with their physical existence. Even under the most severe circumstances, there was no strong motivation to share these meanings with others. When the incorporation of such meanings did occur, the process of interpretation intervened to create a new sensibility that the people identified as arising out of and being connected to their own traditions.

Third, Northern Plains religions did not focus on what Christians would understand as salvation. Even though dangerous and sometimes destructive beings intruded on the worlds of these peoples—with whom they sought to cope through appropriate ritual processes—there was no equivalent of the Christian understanding of a Fall or of the necessity, morally or religiously, to be redeemed from such a condition. To the contrary, the Mandan, Hidatsa, Cheyenne, and Crow religions, as well as other religions on the Northern Plains, were characterized by values that clustered around the flourishing of life in the experienced present. Even though they had the assistance of important culture heroes and creator figures, these persons were not redeemers in the sense of delivering the people from moral evil or religious error.

Northern Plains peoples entertained beliefs about the transition from contemporary human existence to life in the community of the dead, and sometimes individual deeds were related to the quality of one's passage from the land of the living to the land of the dead. But again, such a transition had little to do with the savior figure that is so prominent in Christianity. One certainly had to maintain appropriate relationships, often defined in terms of kinship, between humans and nonhuman powers, but there was no need to be redeemed from moral or natural evil in order to live a productive life or to enter into the land of the dead, there to join one's ancestors.[7]

Fourth, while religions on the Northern Plains were characterized by transcendent nonhuman powers or persons, and while there were often relations among these powers or persons that qualified some as more potent than others, the notion of monotheism is inadequate for interpreting these religions.[8] Monotheism is perhaps best viewed as a construct developed by interpreters of the history of religions who were interested in establishing the difference between the development of Western Christianity and other religions. Rather than appealing to monotheism or similar concepts, students of Native American religion ought to build their understandings on the basis of appeals to specific cultural materials. Such materials, when they are available, can suggest more appropriate terms for interpreting Native American religions.[9]

Fifth, the idea of the supernatural is not adequate to describe the nature of Native American religious experience. The supernatural implies the natural, and the natural as a distinct realm is the construction of cultures that are based on science and that are the heirs of religious traditions, such as Christianity, that give additional support to such a differentiation. Those who make distinctions between the natural world and the supernatural misunderstand not only the religious experiences of Northern Plains peoples but also the experiences of other Native Americans as well. The term *transcendent* is used in this book as a more appropriate term, but even this term does not capture the richness and diversity of Native American religious experience.

Transcendence has the fundamental meaning of *going beyond* the experience of people in their everyday worlds. At the individual level, others transcend the self, memory transcends present experience, and imagination leaps toward visions of the future. In the social world, other groups transcend my group, tradition transcends present experiences that I share with others, and corporate visions of the future transcend present images of group identity. Even though they transcend the everyday world, these experiences arise within that world through the mediation of language and complex symbols.

In the case of Northern Plains peoples, creators, culture heroes, plant and animal beings, and powerful entities such as Thunder, Sun, Moon, and Astral beings also transcended their experience. Through the mediation of symbolic networks embodied in ritual processes, they became richly present in their everyday experience. In addition to sensibilities arising in rituals, these beings were available to be perceived in the everyday world. Sun, Moon, and Astral persons, as well as Thunder and the earth, were clearly a part of everyday experience. The powerful animal and plant persons upon whom particular peoples depended were, in this sense, close at hand. These beings were alive, possessing consciousness and purpose; they spoke to people in their visions and dreams; and they were at the same time availabl: to be experienced as the animals, plants, sun, moon, stars, and earth of the shared world of everyday life.

Finally, these characteristics of past Northern Plains religions are extremely important for understanding the successors of these peoples. Some live on or near their ancestral lands, while others have been moved great distances. Their lives are complicated by the consequences of missionization, the reservation system, and the pervasive poverty, alcoholism, and violence that often mark reservation life. Their triumph over the tragic features of their lives is the result of their capacity for self-renewal, which has often been fueled by their reinterpretation of religious traditions and practices.

Present expressions of Northern Plains religions—whether they involve bundles, pipes, sweat lodges, Sun Dances, or other elements—are not completely disconnected from the distant past described in this book. While they are no longer connected with past forms of economic and social life—buffalo hunting and gardening—they have been reinterpreted in relation to present economic and political problems. In many instances, these religious practices and their informing traditions connect people with their past and give to present experience a sense of continuity with that heritage. But the powers evoked in religious traditions and practices are directed toward the solution of present problems, and the understanding of religion and ritual enactments as having effects in the world of everyday experience continues.

This perspective helps us to understand why Native American religious traditions and practices continue to exist among contemporary Indian peoples. These traditions and practices represent experiential territories that were never conquered by either the invading European cultures or the missionary movements. They persisted and were creatively reinterpreted, and in the process they often assimilated elements from the invading cultures—including aspects of their religion—into their expanding narrative structures.

Even those who formally transferred allegiance from their traditional religions to Christianity often retained many of their inherited traditions and practices, fusing them into new varieties of a distinctly Indian Christianity.

This perspective also helps to explain why a vital and diverse Native American identity remains clearly visible in North American society. The power of Native American religious traditions and practices has continued to stimulate processes of interpretation that have given rise to renewed forms of religious activity that maintain the social identity of these peoples, connecting their identities with memories of predecessors that have not completely been displaced by the predecessors of the invaders. As they resisted extinction in the past, these religiously grounded identities continue into the present and are unlikely to be extinguished in the future. Religious traditions and practices—whether creative innovations or modern expressions based on historical roots—will continue to be important for the identity and persistence of Native American peoples.

NOTES

Introduction

1. Joseph Medicine Crow has acknowledged the general usefulness of such sources for his reconstruction of Crow history. See his book *From the Heart of Crow Country,* ed. Herman J. Viola, Library of the American Indian (New York: Orion Books, 1992), xiv, 9–10. My research on the Blackfeet Reservation in the early 1960s confirmed this view. The documents, photographs, and other holdings of the Museum of the Plains Indian in Browning, Montana, provided the Blackfeet with an essential link to their own past.

2. An interesting contemporary Northern Plains example that illustrates both continuity with the past and assimilation of certain motifs from Christianity is found in Percy Bullchild, *The Sun Came Down: The History of the World as My Black-feet Elders Told It* (San Francisco: Harper and Row, 1985). What is striking about this book is that it presents what is still basically a Blackfeet worldview despite the obvious influences of the missionary movement in both its Protestant and Catholic forms.

3. In this book the terms *Indian* and *Native American* are used interchangeably. The people who now live on Northern Plains reservations typically refer to themselves as Indians when speaking in public spaces to non-natives. Within their own group, the people often refer to themselves by names expressed in their own languages and may identify themselves with the group as a whole or a subgroup.

Chapter 1.   Social Change on the Northern Plains

1. For a general analysis of the two ways of life, see Preston Holder, *The Hoe and the Horse on the Plains: A Study of Cultural Development among North American Indians* (Lincoln: University of Nebraska Press, 1970). Another important treatment is by Symmes C. Oliver, "Ecology and Cultural Continuity as Contributing Factors in the Social Organization of the Plains Indians," *University of California Publications in American Archaeology and Ethnology* 48 (1962): 1 – 90.

2. A very general but helpful treatment of the characteristics of hunting and horticultural societies is found in Gerhard E. Lenski, *Power and Privilege: A Theory of Social Stratification* (Chapel Hill: University of North Carolina Press, 1984), esp. chaps. 5 and 6. ———

3. For descriptions of these trading patterns, see John C. Ewers, "The Indian Trade of the Upper Missouri before Lewis and Clark: An Interpretation," *Bulletin of the Missouri Historical Society* 10/4, pt. 1 (1954): 429 – 46; and W. Raymond Wood, "Plains Trade in Prehistoric and Protohistoric Intertribal Relations," in *Anthropology on the Great Plains,* ed. W. Raymond Wood and Margot Liberty (Lincoln: University of Nebraska Press, 1980), 98 – 109.

4. John C. Ewers, "Was There a Northwestern Plains Sub-Culture? An Ethnographical Appraisal," *Plains Anthropologist* 12, no. 36 (1967): 167 – 70. The three divisions of the Blackfeet to which Ewers refers were the Pikuni, or Piegan; the Kainah, or Blood; and the Siksika, or Northern Blackfeet. After the establishment of a border between the United States and Canada, the southern Piegan remained in Montana, while the northern Piegan, the Bloods, and the Northern Blackfeet were located in the province of Alberta, Canada. Despite geographical redefinition, visiting between relatives and friends among the divisions of the Blackfeet continues to the present day, and important ritual processes that take place in either country are attended by people from both sides of the international border.

5. Clark Wissler, "The Diffusion of Culture in the Plains of North America," *Congrès international des Américanistes,* 15th session (Quebec: Dussault and Prouix, 1907), 2:39 – 52. Wissler was trained in psychology but was attracted to anthropology by the work of Franz Boas.

6. Ibid., 47. See also Leslie Spier, "The Sun Dance of the Plains Indians: Its Development and Diffusion," *Anthropological Papers of the American Museum of Natural History* 16 (1921): 453. Karl Schlesier argues, against Wissler and others, that the Sun Dance originated with the Sutaios, an Algonquian group assimilated by the Cheyennes; see Schlesier, "Rethinking the Midewiwin and the Plains Ceremonial Called the Sun Dance," *Plains Anthropologist* 35, no. 127 (1990): 13.

7. Wissler, "Diffusion of Culture," 47. The reference here to the Atsinas as the Gros Ventres might be confusing because the same name was sometimes used in the literature to refer to the Hidatsas. They were two distinct groups of people. Rather than *Gros Ventres*, I will use the name *Atsinas* to distinguish these people from the Hidatsas.

8. Age-graded societies for men, and sometimes for women, were very widespread among Plains cultures. These societies performed various functions having to do with the assignment of status, the allocation of essential tasks, and the social distribution of power, among other things. Typically, individuals would join an appropriate society in their youth and move through the system until they reached old age. For descriptions of these important social structures, see Robert H. Lowie, "Plains Indian Age-Societies: Historical and Comparative Summary," *Anthropological Papers of the American Museum of Natural History* 11 (1916): 877–992; and Frank H. Stewart, *Fundamentals of Age-Group Systems* (New York: Academic Press, 1977). Stewart's book deals with the Mandans, Hidatsas, Blackfeet, and Atsinas. He provides comparative examples from African groups as well.

9. Wissler, "The Diffusion of Culture," 49. In an essay published in the same volume, A. L. Kroeber argued that the village societies, including the people who became the Crows, were the source from which the age-graded societies diffused among the nomads. See also Frank H. Stewart's conclusions in *Fundamentals of Age-Group Systems*, 329–30.

10. Wissler, "The Diffusion of Culture," 50.

11. Ibid., 51.

12. The Pawnee Hako ritual may be one of the old patterns upon which other pipe ceremonies were built. There is, of course, extensive literature on this issue. See especially the following: Alice C. Fletcher, "The Hako: A Pawnee Ceremony," *Twenty-second Annual Report of the Bureau of American Ethnology*, pt. 2 (1900–1901); George F. Will and George E. Hyde, *Corn among the Indians of the Upper Missouri* (Lincoln: University of Nebraska Press, 1917), 276–78; Jordon Paper, *Offering Smoke: The Sacred Pipe and the Native American Religion* (Moscow, Idaho: University of Idaho Press, 1988), 34–35; Joseph Jablow, *The Cheyenne in Plains Indian Trade Relations, 1795–1840*, American Ethnological Society Monographs, no. 19 (1951), 47–48; W. Raymond Wood, "Plains Trade in Prehistoric and Protohistoric Intertribal Relations" in *Anthropology on the Great Plains*, ed. W. Raymond Wood and Margot Liberty (Lincoln: University of Nebraska Press, 1980), 104–5; John C. Ewers, "Indian Trade"; and Edward M. Bruner, "Mandan," in *Perspectives in American Indian Culture Change*, ed. Edward H. Spicer (Chicago: University of Chicago Press, 1961), 201–2.

13. Robert H. Lowie, "Plains Indian Age-Societies," 948.

14. Clark Wissler, "Comparative Study of Pawnee and Blackfoot Rituals," *Proceedings of the Nineteenth International Congress of Americanists* (1915; Nendeln, Liechtenstein: Kraus Reprint, 1968), 338.

15. Donald J. Lehmer, "The Sedentary Horizon of the Northern Plains," *Southwestern Journal of Anthropology* 10 (1954): 154.

16. Bruner, "Mandan," 205.

17. Holder, *Hoe and Horse*, 226.

18. Alice B. Kehoe, "The Function of Ceremonial Sexual Intercourse among the Northern Plains Indians," *Plains Anthropologist* 15, no. 47 (1970): 99–103.

19. Ibid., 99.

20. Ibid. See also Lowie, "Plains Indian Age-Societies," 949, 951. The Mandan and Hidatsa practice of the sexual transmission of power was commented on widely during the fur trading period. It may well have been that this practice had earlier been confined by social and ritual restraints, as Kehoe has argued. Later, however, under conditions of increasing contact with whites, the practice may have become more widespread and may have been less well integrated into the culture. Such a cultural disintegration could mean, in the case of the women among these groups, the beginning of a more ominous period of sexual exploitation. I discuss this problem in more detail in chapter 5.

21. Kehoe, "Ceremonial Sexual Intercourse," 99.

22. Ibid., 100.

23. Ibid., 101.

24. Ibid., 102.

25. Ibid., 103.

26. Oscar Lewis, *The Effects of White Contact upon Blackfoot Culture, With Special Reference to the Role of the Fur Trade*, Monographs of the American Ethnological Society 6, ed. A. Irving Hallowell (New York: J. J. Augustin, 1942), 36.

27. Ibid.

28. Ibid., 41.

29. Ibid.

30. Ibid.

31. Ceremonial bundles may be defined as a collection of objects, associated with traditions of origin and with ritual processes, that were given under special conditions. A bundle may originate in a dream or a vision occurring in the experience of a historical individual, or its origin may be attributed to a historic predecessor, known or anonymous; to a culture hero; or to some other transcendent power

who typically appears in the form of a person. Bundles pervaded Northern Plains religious thought and practice. See, for example, Clark Wissler, "Ceremonial Bundles of the Blackfoot Indians," *Anthropological Papers of the American Museum of Natural History* 7 (1912): 69–289.

32. Lewis, *Effects,* 45–46.

33. John Ewers, *The Blackfeet: Raiders on the Northwestern Plains.* 49 (Norman: University of Oklahoma Press, 1961), 202.

34. David Mandelbaum, "The Plains Cree," *Anthropological Papers of the American Museum of Natural History* 37 (1940–41): 155–316.

35. On the issue of overtrapping and game depletion, see the interesting and contested analysis by Calvin Martin, *Keepers of the Game: Indian-Animal Relationships and the Fur Trade* (Berkeley: University of California Press, 1978).

36. Mandelbaum, "Plains Cree," 187.

37. Readers who are familiar with this literature will recognize that the sources of change I am dealing with are much discussed. Clearly, the cumulative impact of such things as the horse, the gun, the fur trade, and epidemic disease were critical to understanding how Plains culture evolved. In this chapter I do not deal with these things in themselves but rather I am illustrating how they function in arguments concerning social change among Plains societies.

38. George E. Hyde, *The Early Blackfeet and Their Neighbors,* Old West Series, no. 2 (Denver: John VanMale, 1933), 6. In Hyde's listing, the Amahamis were Hidatsas associated with a particular village. Later archaeological evidence shows that the Mandans would certainly have to be excluded from this list. As Hyde so rightly said, the "spade" often brings arguments to their final conclusion.

39. Ibid., 7. See also the evidence presented in Ewers, *Blackfeet,* 198.

40. Hyde, *Early Blackfeet,* 7.

41. Ibid., 70.

42. Ibid., 8.

43. Ibid. Hyde's view rests on arguments concerning the differences between the Blackfeet language and its eastern variants. Edward Sapir argued that Algonquian-speaking peoples were distributed as far west as the Pacific coast. See Edward Sapir, *Time Perspective in Aboriginal American Culture,* Geological Survey of Canada 13, Anthropological Series (Ottawa, 1916), 81.

44. Frank Raymond Secoy, *Changing Military Patterns on the Great Plains,* Monographs of the American Ethnological Society 21 (New York: J. J. Augustin, 1953). For other classic analyses of the role of the horse in the development of Plains culture, see Clark Wissler, "The Influence of the Horse in the Development of Plains

Culture," *American Anthropologist* 16 (1914): 1–25; and John Ewers, *The Horse in Blackfoot Indian Culture, With Comparative Material from Other Western Tribes.* Smithsonian Institution, Bureau of American Ethnology Bulletin 159 (Washington, D.C., 1955).

45. Secoy, *Changing Military Patterns,* 87.

46. Ibid., 89.

47. Ibid., 90.

48. Ibid.

49. Ibid.

50. Bernard Mishkin, *Rank and Warfare among the Plains Indians,* Monographs of the American Ethnological Society 3 (New York: J. J. Augustin, 1940).

51. Ibid., 12.

52. James Teit, "The Salishan Tribes of the Western Plateaus," ed. Franz Boas, *Forty-fifth Annual Report of the Bureau of American Ethnology,* 45 (1927–28): 151–52.

53. See, for example, Henry F. Dobyns, *Their Number Become Thinned: Native American Population Dynamics in Eastern North America,* Native American Historic Demography Series (Knoxville: University of Tennessee Press, 1983). Schlesier also places a great deal of emphasis on disease as a factor in religious innovation; see "Rethinking the Midewiwin," 1–2.

Chapter 2.   Continuity and Change in Northern Plains Religions

1. This chapter is a synthetic overview of Northern Plains religions. It is constructed on the basis of extensive reading and reflection on Northern Plains societies that I began more than thirty years ago when I first became interested in the Blackfeet. For an elaboration of this approach, see my books *Mission among the Blackfeet,* Civilization of the American Indian Series, vol. 112 (Norman: University of Oklahoma Press, 1971) and *Renewing the World: Plains Indian Religion and Morality* (Tucson: University of Arizona Press, 1987). The theoretical perspective that has informed much of my work is presented in *The Human Center: Moral Agency in the Social World* (Philadelphia: Fortress Press, 1981).

Chapter 3.   Religious Development in the Village Societies

1. The analysis that follows is based on W. Raymond Wood, *An Interpretation of Mandan Culture History,* Smithsonian Institution, Bureau of American Ethnology Bulletin 198 (1967), 117–68. See also Donald J. Lehmer, "The Sedentary Horizon

of the Northern Plains," 139–40; and Alfred W. Bowers, "Chronological Sequences of Missouri River Cultures in the Dakotas" (1935) typescript in Logan Museum of Anthropology, Beloit College, Beloit, Wisconsin. My visits to the Knife River villages, the Huff site, and other archaeological sites around Bismarck, North Dakota, have added to my appreciation of Wood's analysis.

2. Wood, *Mandan Culture History,* 119.

3. Ibid., 131.

4. Ibid., 132.

5. This point becomes important in chapter 6 in establishing a connection between traditions of the Awatixa division of the Hidatsas and the development of certain Cheyenne religious forms. Recent archaeological investigations place at least some of the predecessors of the historical Hidatsas on the Missouri River as early as 1100; see Stanley A. Ahler, Thomas D. Thiessen, and Michael K. Trimble, *People of the Willows: The Prehistory and Early History of the Hidatsa Indians* (Grand Forks: University of North Dakota Press, 1991), 29–30.

6. See W. Raymond Wood and Alan S. Downer, "Notes on the Crow-Hidatsa Schism," *Plains Anthropologist* 22, no. 78, pt. 2, Memoir 13 (1977): 83–100. The process of fissioning was quite widespread on the Northern Plains and affected other village societies as well. An example would be the separation of the Arikaras from the Skidi Pawnees. See James R. Murie, *Ceremonies of the Pawnee,* ed. Douglas R. Parks (1981; reprint, Lincoln: University of Nebraska Press with the American Indian Studies Research Institute, 1989), 29–30.

7. Alfred W. Bowers, *Mandan Social and Ceremonial Organization,* University of Chicago Publications in Anthropology, Social Anthropological Series (Chicago: University of Chicago Press, 1950), 24–25.

8. Alfred W. Bowers, "A History of the Mandan and Hidatsa" (Ph.D. diss., University of Chicago, 1948), 16.

9. White Calf's account is recorded in Bowers, *Mandan,* 347–53. See also the accounts in Martha W. Beckwith, "Mandan-Hidatsa Myths and Ceremonies," *Memoirs of the American Folk-Lore Society* 32 (1938): 1–21; and Maximilian, Prince of Wied, *Travels in the Interior of North America, 1832–1834,* Early Western Travels, 1748–1846, ed. Reuben Gold Thwaites, vol. 23 (Cleveland: Arthur H. Clark Company, 1906), 304–12.

10. Bowers, *Mandan,* 347.

11. The portrayal of important events occurring as a consequence of a wager or some kind of test is widespread. See Robert H. Lowie, "The Test Theme in North American Mythology," *Journal of American Folk-Lore* 21 (1908): 97–148.

12. Bowers, *Mandan,* 280n. 1. According to Bowers, this is the only reference to the image of the world as an earth lodge. This does not detract, however, from the powerful symbolism of the Heart River as the center of the world, an image that is found many other places in these traditions. See, for example, Maximilian, *Travels,* 307. The narrative form of White Calf's version may reflect an incorporation of motifs derived from association with the Christian missionary tradition (the Incarnation, the Virgin Birth), but even if this was the case, the motifs were tightly woven together and dealt clearly with the Mandan creator/culture hero, not the Christian culture hero.

13. Ibid., 156–57. For more autobiographical detail on Wolf Chief, see Carolyn Gilman and Mary Jane Schneider, *The Way to Independence: Memories of a Hidatsa Indian Family, 1840–1920* (St. Paul: Minnesota Historical Society Press, 1987). For additional versions, see Martha Warren Beckwith, "Mandan-Hidatsa Myths and Ceremonies," 10–11; and Maximilian, *Travels,* 312–17.

14. Bowers, *Mandan,* 183.

15. Ibid., 26.

16. W. Raymond Wood, *The Origins of the Hidatsa Indians: A Review of Ethnohistorical and Traditional Data,* Reprints in Anthropology, vol. 32 (Lincoln: J & L Reprint Co., 1986), 27. Wood is repeating the earlier judgment of Bowers; see Bowers, "Mandan and Hidatsa," 1.

17. Wood, *Origins,* 28.

18. Alfred W. Bowers, *Hidatsa Social and Ceremonial Organization,* Smithsonian Institution, Bureau of American Ethnology, Bulletin 194 (Washington, D.C., 1965), 484.

19. Ibid., 298–99.

20. See the account by Butterfly in Wood, *Origins,* 101. This narrative was originally recorded by Gilbert Wilson in 1910.

21. Buffalo Bird Woman's version was recorded by Wilson in his field notes for 1913 and is reproduced in Wood, *Origins,* 110.

22. This fragment appears in Gilbert L. Wilson, "Hidatsa-Mandan Report, Fort Berthold Reservation," typescript in the Minnesota Historical Society, vol. 10 (1911), 309. It would be interesting to know how much gender variation there was in the memorial traditions concerning origins.

23. Bowers, *Hidatsa,* 300–301.

24. Ibid., 303.

25. Ibid., 303–8. See also Wolf Chief's account of Burnt Arrow, recorded in Wilson, "Hidatsa-Mandan Report," vol. 7 (1908), 1–45; and the version by Good Bird in the same volume, pp. 46–70.

26. This tradition served as a charter for the identity of the traditional Hidatsa village and clan structure. As the tradition became more and more complex, with multiple layers of meaning, its core symbolism grew to include the association of the thirteen sky clans with specific parts of an arrow. See the drawing by Bears Arm in Bowers, *Hidatsa*, 292.

27. A Crow version of this narrative appears in Robert H. Lowie, "Myths and Traditions of the Crow Indians," *Anthropological Papers of the American Museum of Natural History* 25 (1922): 74–85. Interestingly, in this tradition the evil being was a woman.

28. Bowers, *Hidatsa*, 323.

29. Ibid. These female figures were associated with important bundles and ritual processes discussed in the next chapter. In addition, men who dreamed of Village Old Woman, as well as certain of the other female figures, were considered destined to become berdaches, the third gender in Northern Plains societies.

30. Bowers, *Hidatsa*, 338. For a version of this tradition, see Bowers, *Mandan*, 197–205.

31. Bowers, *Mandan*, 197–205. For the Hidatsa version, see Bowers, *Hidatsa*, 333–38. The Good Bear version is similar to the Sweet Medicine tradition of the Cheyennes, discussed in chapter 6.

32. Bowers, *Mandan*, 198.

Chapter 4. Religious Organizations and Ritual Processes

1. The description that follows relies mainly on George Catlin, *O-Kee-Pa: A Religious Ceremony, and Other Customs of the Mandans*, ed. John C. Ewers (New Haven: Yale University Press, 1967), 39–85; and Bowers, *Mandan*, 111–63. Rather than following Catlin's spelling, I have adopted the more common rendering *Okipa*. An interesting recent "reading" of Catlin's text informed by postmodernist perspectives is found in an analysis by Vincent Crapanzano: "Hermes' Dilemma: The Masking of Subversion in Ethnographic Description," in *Writing Culture: The Poetics and Politics of Ethnography; A School of American Research Advanced Seminar*, ed. James Clifford and George E. Marcus (Berkeley: University of California Press, 1986), 53–60.

2. The songs of the Okipa ritual memorialized, in historical order from ancient to more recent, the names and locations of past Mandan villages on the Missouri River between the Knife and Grand Rivers; see Bowers, "Missouri River Cultures," 2–3.

3. Bowers, *Mandan*, 111.

4. Ibid., 121–22.

5. Ibid., 118–20.

6. Ibid., 349–51.

7. Ibid., 359–60. In another tradition related by White Calf, four turtles at the bottom of the ocean were supporting the world on their backs; ibid., 350.

8. Catlin, *O-Kee-Pa*, 59.

9. Ibid., 85.

10. Ibid., 69.

11. Power was transmitted sexually not only in the Okipa but also in the age societies that individuals joined. The men who joined a society offered their wives to older men as a part of the membership rite, and through this process both husband and wife partook of the older man's power. This theme was introduced in chapter 1 and is taken up again in the next chapter in connection with buffalo-calling rituals shared by the Mandans and Hidatsas.

12. Catlin, *O-Kee-Pa*, 58. The illustrations that accompany this edition represent in a graphic manner the torture features of the Okipa.

13. Ibid., 64. A more practical reason for tying the foreskins of the sufferers may have been to prevent a possible loss of urine during the period when they were rendered unconscious.

14. The evidence concerning other observations of the Okipa is summarized by John Ewers in his introduction to Catlin's text; see *O-Kee-Pa*, 25–33. The important aspects of Ewers's summary include the following points.

Twenty-six years after Catlin witnessed the Mandan Okipa, Henry Boller, a clerk at Fort Atkinson, observed part of the ritual, although he apparently did not see the events of the last day. In Boller's account, women cleaned the plaza in preparation for the ritual, and an old medicine man, Black Eagle, opened the ceremony. He was naked except for a white wolf robe, his body was painted red, and he wore wolf skin around each ankle. The torture features described in this account seem typical, with the exception that the young men attached themselves to poles that were outside the Okipa lodge itself. This account agrees with Catlin that the skewers must be torn from the flesh, and Boller says that, in order to accomplish this, some of the men had to be suspended with extra weight, which was provided by buffalo skulls attached to skewers in their arms and legs. The "last race" occurred in the same general form as in Catlin's description, although Boller says that sometimes a sufferer had to wait until the flesh around the splints rotted before he was released. The "feast of the buffaloes," was not included in Boller's account.

The last known description of the Okipa by an eyewitness came from Lieutenant Henry E. Maynadier, who observed the ritual in August 1860. His account included the same general features as Boller's and Catlin's, except that in this case a woman was present at the beginning of the ritual along with the leading medicine man. This woman was in mourning, her body was scarified, and she lamented the death of one of her relatives. This is the first time a motif such as this appears, although it may have been present and not described by others. Maynadier's account also describes the sufferers being tied to poles outside the lodge or suspended on scaffolds. At the end of the ritual, all of the objects that were used were placed inside an area surrounded with planks. This structure encircled the sacred cedar that stood at the center of the village plaza.

Two other accounts tend to confirm Catlin's general description. Lewis Henry Morgan, writing in 1862 on the basis of a report from a young eyewitness, confirmed the presence of a Trickster/Clown figure replete with body paint and an enormous penis. Washington Matthews, an army surgeon who was at Fort Buford near Like-a-Fishhook village from 1869 to 1872, said that the village still had a central plaza, an Okipa lodge, and the cedar. Maximilian does not provide much in the way of new detail in his description of the Okipa. He omits any reference to the sexual activities of the Trickster/Clown figure, and he does not describe the "feast of the buffaloes," but his description includes the same general features found in the other accounts.

15. Bowers, *Mandan,* 184–87. Bowers discusses the complex memories surrounding these bundles. Some said that long ago both had been kept together and the ritual had been performed by one man. Later the Skull bundle became associated with one Mandan village and the Robe bundle with another. My analysis deals only with the Robe bundle in this context. For Bowers's treatment, see *Mandan,* 187–90.

16. The following description is largely derived from Will and Hyde, *Corn among the Indians,* 244, 262–68.

17. Bowers, *Mandan,* 193.

18. Ibid., 194.

19. The next chapter includes a more extensive discussion of gender and a further elaboration of the understanding of social status and power operating here.

20. Bowers analyzes the term *Naxpike* as follows: "This is an abbreviation of *nax'pi* meaning 'hide,' *ni'ki* which means to strike, and *hE* meaning 'this act or event' "; *Mandan,* 308. See also the description by Robert H. Lowie in "The Hidatsa Sun Dance," *Anthropological Papers of the American Museum of Natural History* 16 (1921).

21. Schlesier, "Rethinking the Midewiwin," 13.

22. Leslie Spier described the complex differences as well as the formal similarities among Plains Sun Dances. He also concluded that *Sun Dance* was actually a misnomer, since for individual groups many other motifs were often more important than the sun. See Leslie Spier, "The Sun Dance of the Plains Indians: Its Development and Diffusion," *Anthropological Papers of the American Museum of Natural History* 16 (1921).

23. Bowers, *Hidatsa,* 308

24. The description that follows depends for its details on Bowers's analysis in *Hidatsa,* 308–23.

25. The bundle's power did not reside in the material objects alone, since they could be duplicated, but was released through the enactment of the ritual process. However, since it was not duplicated, the sacred ax of Long Arm is an example of an object in which materiality and potency were associated in an indistinguishable manner.

26. Lowie, "The Hidatsa Sun Dance," 416.

27. During this period the person who ritually assumed the identity of Long Arm in the Naxpike was an individual named Porcupine Pemmican; see Bowers, *Hidatsa,* 309.

28. Ibid., 314.

29. For a description of the social role of the berdache in the Crow Sun Dance, see Robert H. Lowie, "The Sun Dance of the Crow Indians," *Anthropological Papers of the American Museum of Natural History* 16 (1921): 29–35.

30. Other elements of the Naxpike evoked enemy symbolism as well. For example, after the lodge was constructed, a small post was erected in the shelter. This post, representing an enemy, was dressed in fine clothing, which included a quill-work robe. Four warriors entered the lodge and attacked the "enemy," stripping the post of the clothing. The first warrior to strike the post took the robe, and the other three divided the clothing, which they then proceeded to give away to old men standing outside the lodge. Bowers, *Hidatsa,* 316.

31. Lowie, "The Hidatsa Sun Dance," 307.

32. Ibid., 422. This structure resembled that constructed by the Crows for their Sun Dance. See Lowie, "The Sun Dance of the Crow," 38–39; see also Fred Miller, "The Crow Sun Dance Lodge: Form, Process, and Geometry in the Creation of Sacred Space," *Temenos* 16 (1960): 92–102.

33. The reference here is to the consequences attributed to the visits of Maximilian and Catlin in the 1830s. Because Catlin was viewed as possessing special

powers, he gained admission to the Okipa. He not only observed the ritual but also painted a number of very explicit scenes in the Okipa lodge. In 1851, Rudolph Friederick Kurz was driven out of the Mandan-Hidatsa village because the people believed that an outbreak of cholera was caused by his painting of village scenes. Bowers, "Mandan and Hidatsa," 135–36.

Chapter 5.   Religious Continuity and Change in the Village Societies

1. Bowers, *Hidatsa,* 374–75.

2. Schlesier, among others, has argued that the development of both the Midewiwin and the Sun Dance are best interpreted as revitalization movements that arose in response to European encroachment and the spread of epidemic diseases; see "Rethinking the Midewiwin," 1. For estimates of population reductions among the Plains Indians due to disease, see Robert H. Lowie, *Indians of the Plains* (Lincoln: University of Nebraska Press, 1982), 10–11. Among the Mandans, as well as other Northern Plains groups, the smallpox epidemic of 1781–82 initiated changes that became more extensive as a consequence of the outbreak of 1837.

3. Bruner, "Mandan," 213. Population estimates vary widely, with some of the lowest placing the Mandan population at only thirty in the spring of 1837.

4. Ibid., 187.

5. Ibid., 230–32. Bruner also notes that there were thirteen Mandan clans in 1750. After the epidemic of 1781–82 only nine remained, and by 1862 the number had declined to four.

6. Ibid., 233.

7. Ibid., 188.

8. W. P. Clark, *The Indian Sign Language* (Philadelphia, 1885), 428, 434, cited in Bruner, "Mandan," 231.

9. Bowers, *Hidatsa,* 36.

10. Bowers, "Mandan and Hidatsa," 138.

11. Ibid., 143–44.

12. Ibid., 147–48.

13. Ibid., 148.

14. Bowers, *Hidatsa,* 281.

15. Ibid., 154.

16. Lowie, "The Hidatsa Sun Dance," 416.

17. Ibid., 415. As late as 1917 the Mandans and Hidatsas vehemently denied any connection between the Okipa and the Naxpike. Even though neither ritual had been enacted for some time and existed only as a part of the memorial tradition in 1917, people still viewed them as central to their self-understanding and as deeply associated with their social identity.

18. Some of these factors were mentioned by the interpreters analyzed in chapter 1.

19. A book that deals with visionary traditions on the Great Plains as a whole was published after this study was completed. For comparative material, see Lee Irwin, *The Dream Seekers: Native American Visionary Traditions of the Great Plains,* Civilization of the American Indian series, vol. 213 (Norman: University of Oklahoma Press, 1994).

20. Bowers, *Hidatsa,* 287.

21. Ibid., 48. As mentioned in chapter 1, there was widespread bilingualism among the village society population, which made such contacts productive for both parties.

22. Ibid., 49.

23. The description that follows is found in Wilson, "Hidatsa-Mandan Report," vol. 16 (1914), 58–110.

24. Bowers claimed that the date of this transfer was about 1870; see *Hidatsa,* 91. I arrived at the date of 1880–81 on the basis of the statement by Wolf Chief, who was born in about 1849, that he was thirty-two years old when the Grass Dance was transferred; Wilson, "Hidatsa-Mandan Report," vol. 16 (1914), 58. Even though Bowers interpreted this transfer as evidence of the breakdown of the traditional age groups in Hidatsa society, it still illustrates a social practice that was widespread in earlier times.

25. Wilson, "Hidatsa-Mandan Report," vol. 16 (1914), 83.

26. Bowers, *Hidatsa,* 175.

27. Wilson, "Hidatsa-Mandan Report," vol. 16 (1914), 60–61.

28. Ibid., 9.

29. The Grass Dance transferred to the Hidatsa and Mandan young men was also transferred in the same year to the Crows, which meant that both groups could share in the benefits of the ritual; see Bowers, *Hidatsa,* 92.

30. Bowers, *Hidatsa,* 167.

31. For a comparative overview of the ritual processes shared by the Mandans and Hidatsas, see Bowers's table in *Mandan,* 20. This table is based on data that Bowers gathered from individuals who remembered a largely nineteenth-century

cultural situation that was probably much more integrated than it was earlier. Thus the large number of cultural items that appeared in Bowers's table represent the end of a process of gradual cultural integration and incorporation of these ritual similarities through the process of reinterpretation. The Mandans and Hidatsas shared other ritual processes that surrounded activities (such as fish and eagle trapping) and important natural or animal others (such as Thunder and Grizzly Bear). Rather than analyzing all of these materials, a more detailed discussion of bundles and rituals surrounding hunting and agriculture will serve to illustrate the development of formal similarities at the level of ritual performance. Beneath these similarities were complex symbolic meanings that were quite distinct and that functioned to preserve the sense of group identity.

32. Bowers, *Mandan,* 117–18.

33. Bowers, *Hidatsa,* 434–35.

34. Ibid., 434.

35. Ibid., 438.

36. For example, the Buffalo Corral and Buffalo Neckbone rituals were shared by both groups; Bowers, *Mandan,* 20.

37. Bowers, *Hidatsa,* 438.

38. A Blood Clot figure appears in the Blackfeet tradition. See Clark Wissler and D. C. Duvall, "Blackfoot Mythology," *Anthropological Papers of the American Museum of Natural History* 2 (1908): 53–58. An individual called Blood Man also appears in the Buffalo Corral ritual of the Hidatsas; see Bowers, *Hidatsa,* 446.

39. Bowers indicated that this ritual was observed by Lewis and Clark as well as Maximilian; see *Hidatsa,* 451.

40. Ibid., 452.

41. Bowers, *Mandan,* 20. Mandan and Hidatsa traditions of the origin of the Red Stick ritual exhibited considerable internal variation as well as differences from one another. Given the material that has been gathered on the ritual, the variation seems more pronounced for the Hidatsas than for the Mandans, but there is no way to determine whether the existing variations are the only ones or whether there were others that were not recorded.

42. Corn Silk in this tradition was not associated with the person of the same name in the Good Furred Robe tradition.

43. Bowers, *Mandan,* 315–16.

44. Bowers, *Hidatsa,* 452–54.

45. Ibid., 454.

46. Ibid.

47. The Mandans have another ritual, the Snow Owl, that involved similar sexual transfers of power; see Bowers, *Mandan,* 282–95.

48. Bowers, *Mandan,* 317–18.

49. Bowers, *Hidatsa,* 455–61.

50. Ibid., 463. The evidence is unclear on the question of whether women had the right to refuse to participate in sexual transfers of power when the negotiations took place primarily between men. Some of the examples seem to suggest that in earlier times accepted norms shaped the behavior of both men and women. If this is true, then refusal to participate would have been very serious since relationships with transcendent powers were at stake. Later, however, the meaning of refusing to participate may have changed, as some of these examples seem to indicate.

51. Ibid., 199. The Goose society, a women's society related to agriculture, was also transferred from the Mandans to the Hidatsas.

52. Ibid., 205; Bowers, *Mandan,* 325–26.

53. Bowers, *Hidatsa,* 205–6.

54. Bowers, *Mandan,* 327.

55. Bowers, *Hidatsa,* 200–207.

56. In both Mandan and Hidatsa societies, the power of women was also grounded in their ownership of the lodge, the household equipment, and the gardens.

57. Ibid., 205. It will be interesting to reflect further on these issues when, later in the chapter, we discuss the Goose society, since in this case the view was that menstrual flows were good for the gardens.

58. Ibid., 339.

59. Bowers, *Mandan,* 188–89.

60. Ibid., 185.

61. Bowers, *Hidatsa,* 333.

62. Bowers, *Mandan,* 198; Bowers, *Hidatsa,* 336.

63. Bowers, *Mandan,* 198; Bowers, *Hidatsa,* 336.

64. Bowers, *Mandan,* 202; Bowers, *Hidatsa,* 335.

65. Bowers, *Mandan,* 184.

66. Ibid. 200. These ingenious images illustrate some of the many elements of humor that characterized these narratives.

67. Ibid., 200–205; Bowers, *Hidatsa,* 333–38. A tradition involving the command not to dig up a turnip is also present among the Blackfeet; see Wissler and Duvall, "Blackfoot Mythology," 58–61. For a Crow version, see Lowie, "Myths and Traditions of the Crow," 52–57.

68. The description that follows is based on Bowers, *Hidatsa,* 204–7.

Chapter 6.   Religious Transformations on the Northern Plains

1. Again it must be emphasized that the development of the Mandans and Hidatsas as peoples needs to be interpreted as a dynamic process involving social evolution and fundamental social change along the way. The shift in perspective in this chapter is not meant to introduce a new problem but rather to focus attention on the transformative features of religion among a range of other peoples on the Northern Plains.

2. One type of analysis could appeal to comparative material on several differ-ent groups. The other, which I have chosen, deals with fewer groups. Actually, these two approaches are complementary, at least in theory, and could be pursued to-gether. Although a broader comparative study might provide greater scope, the detailed complexity of the approach pursued here provides theoretical and meth-odological perspectives that might inform broader studies.

3. The problem that preoccupied many of the earlier interpreters—namely, the question of the extent to which Plains culture arose as a consequence of the diffusion of institutions and practices from the village societies—is redefined here to focus specifically on religion. Another study would be required to explore the broader implications of the earlier interpretations.

4. For an analysis of the problems surrounding the question of when the Crows separated from the Hidatsas, see W. Raymond Wood and Alan S. Downer, "Notes on the Crow-Hidatsa Schism," *Plains Anthropologist* 22, no. 78, pt. 2, Memoir 13 (1977): 83–100. This study provides a summary of both the linguistic and the ethnohistorical evidence. There is no consensus on the details of the separation; I have made my judgments on the basis of a careful reading of the sources. See also Jeffery R. Hanson, "Ethnohistorical Problems in the Crow-Hidatsa Separation," *Archaeology in Montana* 20 (1979): 73–86; and W. Raymond Wood, *The Origins of the Hidatsa Indians: A Review of Ethnohistorical and Traditional Data*, Reprints in Anthropology, vol. 32 (Lincoln, Nebr.: J & L Reprint Co., 1986), 28. The migrating peoples who became the Crows were also divided into three groups, which may have separated from the Hidatsas at different times. For a discussion of the three divi-sions, see Robert H. Lowie, *The Crow Indians* (New York: Farrar & Rinehart, 1935), 4–5.

5. For example, the Hidatsas understood the Grandson narratives in relation to the Charred Body Tradition, and the Crows integrated Grandson into their own developing traditions; see Robert H. Lowie, "Studies in Plains Indian Folklore," *University of California Publications in American Archaeology and Ethnology* 40 (1942– 53): 1–28. The traditional Crow Sun Dance, which was last performed in about

1875, may have developed out of motifs that were present in the Hidatsa Naxpike. Another religious development occurred in 1941 when the Crows incorporated a version of the Sun Dance from the Wind River Shoshones; see Fred W. Voget, *The Shoshoni-Crow Sun Dance* (Norman: University of Oklahoma Press, 1984).

6. Robert H. Lowie, "Myths and Traditions of the Crow Indians," *Anthropological Papers of the American Museum of Natural History* 25 (1922): 15. Medicine Crow was a Crow chief and one of Lowie's important sources of cultural information. For additional details, see the account in Robert H. Lowie, *Crow Indians,* 122–31; and the version recorded by S. C. Simms, *Traditions of the Crows,* Publications of the Field Museum of Natural History, Anthropological Series, vol. 2, no. 6 (Chicago, 1903), 281–82. Simms's account, based on a rendition by Bull That Goes Hunting, contains no reference to either stars or tobacco.

7. Lowie, "Myths and Traditions of the Crow," 272. See also Robert H. Lowie, "The Tobacco Society of the Crow Indians," *Anthropological Papers of the American Museum of Natural History* 21 (1920): 177.

8. See Bowers, *Hidatsa,* 301–2; Wood, *Origins of the Hidatsa,* 97; and Lowie, "Tobacco Society," 177. Lowie's version of the tradition tells of the separation of two brothers, one of whom was destined to live by the corn, squash, and medicine pipe (Hidatsas), and the other of whom was destined to live by tobacco (Crows). The tobacco plant cultivated in connection with the Tobacco society was not smoked. When the plants were mature, their seeds were gathered for the next season, and the remainder of the plant was cut up and thrown into a creek or river. In a contemporary version of the tradition, Joseph Medicine Crow says that the separation was led by a chief named No Vitals. While No Vitals and another chief, named Red Scout, were fasting on the shore of Devil's Lake, each had a vision. Red Scout received an ear of corn in his vision, while No Vitals received a pod of sacred seeds (tobacco). See Medicine Crow, *Crow Country,* 19–20.

9. Not all groups that became farmers in the course of their migrations altogether abandoned their agricultural traditions during their evolution into horse nomads. Crow people did not lose their taste for garden produce and some continued to visit the Hidatsas to obtain vegetable foods.

10. Lowie, "Tobacco Society," 114. The description of the Tobacco society in this chapter generally follows Lowie. See also Lowie, *Crow Indians,* chap. 15; S. C. Simms, "Cultivation of 'Medicine Tobacco' by the Crows: A Preliminary Paper," *American Anthropologist,* n.s., 6 (1904): 331–35; and my earlier description in *Renewing the World,* 108–13.

11. Lowie, "Tobacco Society," 117.

12. Ibid., 195. Lowie argued that women participated in significant ways in all of the major ritual processes in Crow society.

13. Ibid., 144.

14. On the Crow Sun Dance, see Lowie, "Sun Dance of the Crow," and Lowie, *Crow Indians,* chap. 16. For additional religious practices, see also Robert H. Lowie, "The Religion of the Crow Indians," *Anthropological Papers of the American Museum of Natural History* 25 (1922): 309–444. And for a discussion focusing particularly on bundles, see William Wildschut, *Crow Indian Medicine Bundles,* ed. John Ewers, Contributions from the Museum of the American Indian, Heye Foundation 17 (New York, 1960).

15. Bowers, *Hidatsa,* 300, 302. Other Northern Plains societies, such as the Blackfeet, planted tobacco gardens, but none of them developed the equivalent of the Crow Tobacco society.

16. For representative discussions of Cheyenne migrations, see George Bird Grinnell, *The Cheyenne Indians: Their History and Ways of Life* (Lincoln: University of Nebraska Press, 1972), 1:1–46; George E. Hyde, *Life of George Bent Written from His Letters* (Norman: University of Oklahoma Press, 1968), chap. 1; E. Adamson Hoebel, *The Cheyennes: Indians of the Great Plains,* 2d ed., Case Studies in Cultural Anthropology (New York: Holt, Rinehart and Winston, 1978), 4–11; Karl Schlesier, *The Wolves of Heaven: Cheyenne Shamanism, Ceremonies, and Prehistoric Origins,* Civilization of the American Indian series, vol. 183 (Norman: University of Oklahoma Press, 1987); and W. Raymond Wood, *Biesterfeldt: A Post-Contact Coalescent Site on the Northeastern Plains,* Smithsonian Contributions to Anthropology 15 (Washington, D.C.: Smithsonian Institution Press, 1971), 51–68. In his book *The Cheyenne Nation: A Social and Demographic History* (Lincoln: University of Nebraska Press, 1987), 78, John H. Moore has provided the most complete and detailed analysis of Cheyenne development to date. On the basis of a study of early maps, he demonstrates that there is little doubt that Cheyennes once lived in the vicinity of Leech Lake in Minnesota.

17. Wood, *Biesterfeldt,* 67.

18. Grinnell, *Cheyenne Indians,* 1:21–22.

19. Hoebel, *Cheyennes,* 9–11. Although I consider the Cheyenne Sun Dance to be an important identity-forming institution, it is not at the center of attention in this analysis. See my treatment in *Renewing the World,* 141–52.

20. Wood, *Biesterfeldt,* 67.

21. Moore, *Cheyenne Nation,* 69. Cf. Grinnell, *Cheyenne Indians,* 1:253.

22. Moore, *Cheyenne Nation,* 100.

23. That summary, like this one, relies on Bowers, *Hidatsa,* 303–8.

24. Three points need to be made about these oral traditions. First, it is impossible to date with certainty the origin of the Charred Body tradition; this problem must be extended to the Cheyenne tradition as well. As was also the case for many major narratives, several versions of each of these traditions were probably circulating among the various groups prior to historical contact. The same observation can be made for the historical Hidatsas and Cheyennes, although the main elements of these two traditions still formed a coherent core of meaning shared by each group. In addition, these traditions may have evolved from relatively simple plot structures, becoming more and more complex as new experiences required creative additions to the narratives.

Second, since it is not likely that these traditions can be dated accurately, it is probably impossible to identify their ultimate communities of origin with certainty. Thus the question of whether the Charred Body tradition became a creative source of the symbolic forms that provided identity and direction to ancestral Awatixas in their religious and cultural development cannot be answered with absolute finality. Elements of this tradition figured prominently in the historical Hidatsa Sun Dance, and it is at least plausible that this tradition played a creative role in the earlier development of these people. In the case of the Cheyennes, however, it is possible to make a stronger case that the Sweet Medicine tradition embodied powerful symbolic meanings that were essential to the movement of these groups from a status of semisedentary gardeners to that of a fully nomadic hunting people.

Third, despite these problems, none of the other groups who came to occupy the Northern Plains during historical times had origin or culture hero traditions in which arrow symbolism played such a central role. There were various arrow motifs among other groups, to be sure, but none of them were mediated through complex traditions associated with such culturally important predecessors.

25. Given their previous association with the Hidatsas, it is not surprising that the Crows had a bundle that embodied arrow symbolism as well; see Wildschut, *Crow Indian Medicine Bundles,* 48–51.

26. Some of the important sources of this tradition are the following: George Bird Grinnell, "Some Early Cheyenne Tales II," *Journal of American Folk-Lore* 21 (1908): 269–320; George A. Dorsey, "Ceremonial Organization," in *The Cheyenne,* Field Columbian Museum, Anthropological Series 1 (Chicago, 1905), 41–46; Richard W. Randolph, *Sweet Medicine* (Caldwell, Idaho: Caxton Printers, 1937), 11–17. For more recent treatments, see Peter J. Powell, *Sweet Medicine* (Norman: Uni-

versity of Oklahoma Press, 1969), 2:460–66; and Moore, *The Cheyenne Nation,* 103–5. Moore has considerable insight into the problems that surrounded the gathering of these traditions, as well as the difficulties that accompany efforts to interpret them.

27. Grinnell, *Cheyenne Indians,* 2:345.

28. While this version of the tradition may reflect missionary contact, echoing the story of the loaves and fishes in the Gospel of Luke, the core elements remained culturally consistent with the Cheyenne social identity. The tradition also recalls the inexhaustible pot of mush of the Old Woman Who Never Dies. Also, one of the young men she fed was named Sweet Medicine.

29. The symbolic representation of reciprocal relations between male and female figures in this narrative is interesting since the arrow ritual developed in such a way that women were largely excluded from participation, and the power of the arrows was focused on the male activities of hunting and warfare; see Hoebel, *Cheyennes,* 14–18. If, as I argue in this chapter, the arrow ritual and Sweet Medicine were essential to the move from agriculture to hunting, then such a development might be expected.

30. See my description of these functions in *Renewing the World,* 102–8.

31. If Sweet Medicine was a historical figure, this charismatic individual may have reimagined past Cheyenne traditions, combining them with elements he found in the surrounding environment. Whether this happened or whether the Sweet Medicine tradition was the product of another individual's creative religious imagination, an interaction with the Awatixa narrative seems likely.

32. Harold N. Ottaway, "A Possible Origin for the Cheyenne Sacred Arrow Complex," *Plains Anthropologist* 15, no. 47 (1970): 96.

33. Schlesier, "Rethinking the Midewiwin," 16–17.

34. Ibid., 16.

35. Moore, *Cheyenne Nation,* 100–101. Moore argues that the tradition that reflected the uniting of these two groups was a narrative about two young men who entered a spring and encountered an old woman who showed them fields of corn and herds of buffalo. After this revelation, the buffalo came out of the spring as food for the people, and they also began to grow corn. It is significant that the names of these two young men were Red Red Red and Corn Leaf, the former being associated with the bloody hunt and the latter with the plant world. The Sweet Medicine tradition constituted these two bands as a political entity, the Cheyenne nation.

36. Ibid., 121. Moore's analysis is very complex. He argues that there was a tradition of a conflict between Sweet Medicine and a culture hero named Lime that

documented the shared memory of the assimilation of the Sutaios. In this tradition, Sweet Medicine and Lime engaged in a shaman's battle. After each one killed the other, he was healed by mysterious powers. Finally it became clear that neither culture hero could defeat the other, at which point they agreed to join together and make peace. For a previously unpublished version of the Lime tradition, see Moore, *Cheyenne Nation,* 109–13. For a later history of the Sutaio band, see ibid., 232–34.

37. Bowers, *Hidatsa,* 21. See also Wood, *Origins,* 31. Wood follows Bowers in his analysis.

38. The description that follows relies on Bowers, *Hidatsa,* 348–63. Some of these bundles contained sacred arrows, while others did not.

39. Bowers, *Hidatsa,* 350.

40. In addition to being bilingual, many Northern Plains people were quite adept at imitating and reproducing the songs, movements, objects, and body painting associated with particular bundle rituals.

41. The plausibility of my argument depends on when particular groups of Cheyennes were on the Missouri River. If Moore is correct that the Aortas and the Eaters were constituted as a people by the Sweet Medicine tradition around 1720, then the Awaxawi-Cheyenne interaction at Fort Yates receives some support. It may also be true that the arrow symbolism and ritual process were present in earlier Cheyenne traditions. In this case, the suggestion that they formed this tradition when they were in association with groups of Hidatsas before they reached the river also seems possible. In the final analysis, it is impossible to prove whether the Sweet Medicine tradition was *created* as a consequence of interactions with the Hidatsas, or whether this tradition was creatively *expanded* by contact with the Charred Body narrative. While my analysis is biased toward the first alternative, the actual historical process was probably more complex.

42. John Moore, "A Study of Religious Symbolism among the Cheyenne Indians" (Ph.D. diss., New York University, 1974), 211–13.

43. Ibid., 214.

44. I am not arguing here that the Sweet Medicine tradition was the *only* tradition or ritual process that constituted what later became the Cheyenne identity. Certainly the Sun Dance and other complex rituals were finally important for understanding this broader picture. What I am arguing is that the Sweet Medicine tradition and the Sacred Arrow bundle were critical to the *beginning* of the process. On this point I agree with Moore and disagree with Schlesier, who identifies the Massaum, an animal dance that some have compared with aspects of the Mandan Okipa, as the central identity-forming institution among the Cheyennes. See Schle-

sier, *Wolves of Heaven,* chap. 5. Schlesier associates this institution with the founding narrative of Yellow Haired Woman, or Ehyophstah, which I discuss in *Renewing the World,* 94–99.

45. Once constructed, these social worlds persisted into the present, though they were not unchanged. The history of the changes, such as the division between the southern and northern Cheyennes, is not the subject of this analysis. Rather, I am trying to identify the essential features in the religious life of these peoples that provided the social energy to transform themselves and evolve new identities.

Chapter 7.   American Indian Religions
             and the Construction of Cultures

1. The classic source for understanding the power of religion to shape the identity of entire societies is, of course, Emile Durkheim. See especially *The Elementary Forms of the Religious Life: A Study in Religious Sociology* (London: George Allen & Unwin, 1915). There has been much discussion of civil religion in America, and the indispensable source that stimulated considerable research is Robert Bellah, "Civil Religion in America," *Daedalus* 96 (1967): 1–21.

2. See Sam Gill's discussion of this point in *Native American Religions: An Introduction,* The Religious Life of Man series (Belmont, Calif.: Wadsworth Publishing Company, 1982), 44–45.

3. In many instances, Native American healing practices were also infused with religious meanings. For a recent overview, see Åke Hultkrantz, *Shamanic Healing and Ritual Drama: Health and Medicine in Native North American Religious Traditions,* Health/Medicine and the Faith Traditions series (New York: Crossroad, 1992).

4. The performative nature of Native American religions is discussed by Sam Gill in *Native American Religious Action: A Performance Approach to Religion,* Studies in Comparative Religion (Columbia: University of South Carolina Press, 1987).

5. The literature on this point is extensive. For representative treatments, see James Axtell, *The Invasion Within: The Contest of Cultures in Colonial North America,* Cultural Origins of North America series, no. 1 (New York: Oxford University Press, 1985); Karen Anderson, *Chain Her by One Foot: The Subjugation of Women in Seventeenth-Century New France* (New York: Routledge, 1991), a fascinating study of the missionary impact on gender relations in New France; Kenneth M. Morrison, "Discourse and the Accommodation of Values: Toward a Revision of Mission History," *Journal of the American Academy of Religion* 53 (1985): 365–82; and my book, *Mission among the Blackfeet* (Norman: University of Oklahoma Press, 1971), as well

as my essay "Missionary Life-World and Native Response: Jesuits in New France," *Sciences Religieuses/Studies in Religion* 13 (1984): 179–92.

6. Native American peoples did not consider their religions to be universal, which is the form that most versions of missionary Christianity took.

7. Certainly this general view changed as contact with Christian missionaries increased. For a representative discussion of the influence of missionization on views of the dead and the afterlife, see Åke Hultkrantz, "The Problem of Christian Influence on Northern Algonkian Eschatology," in his book *Belief and Worship in Native North America* (Ithaca, N. Y.: Syracuse University Press, 1981) chap. 11.

8. The work of Åke Hultkrantz illustrates the problems that arise when interpretive appeals are made to the notion of monotheism; see, for example, Hultkrantz, *The Religions of the American Indians,* Hermeneutics, Studies in the History of the American Indians (Berkeley: University of California Press, 1979), chap. 2, pp. 15–26; and *Belief and Worship,* chap. 2, pp. 20–26.

9. My interpretation has not, of course, completely avoided the problems entailed in such terminology.

BIBLIOGRAPHY

Ahler, Stanley A., Thomas D. Thiessen, and Michael K. Trimble. *People of the Willows: The Prehistory and Early History of the Hidatsa Indians.* Grand Forks: University of North Dakota Press, 1991.

Anderson, Karen. *Chain Her by One Foot: The Subjugation of Women in Seventeenth-Century New France.* New York: Routledge, 1991.

Axtell, James. *The Invasion Within: The Contest of Cultures in Colonial North America.* Cultural Origins of North America series, no. 1. New York: Oxford University Press, 1985.

Beckwith, Martha Warren. "Mandan-Hidatsa Myths and Ceremonies." *Memoirs of the American Folk-Lore Society* 32 (1938).

Bellah, Robert. "Civil Religion in America." *Daedalus* 96 (1967): 1–21.

Bowers, Alfred W. "Chronological Sequences of Missouri River Cultures in the Dakotas." Logan Museum of Anthropology, Beloit College, Beloit, Wis. Typescript, 1935.

———. Correspondence and Papers. Logan Museum of Anthropology, Beloit College, Beloit, Wis.

———. *Hidatsa Social and Ceremonial Organization.* Smithsonian Institution, Bureau of American Ethnology Bulletin 194. Washington, D.C., 1965.

———. "A History of the Mandan and Hidatsa." Ph.D. diss., University of Chicago, 1948.

————. *Mandan Social and Ceremonial Organization.* University of Chicago Publications in Anthropology, Social Anthropological Series. Chicago: University of Chicago Press, 1950.

Bruner, Edward M. "Mandan." In *Perspectives in American Indian Culture Change*, ed. Edward H. Spicer, 187–277. Chicago: University of Chicago Press, 1961.

Bullchild, Percy. *The Sun Came Down: The History of the World as My Blackfeet Elders Told It.* San Francisco: Harper & Row, 1985.

Catlin, George. *Letters and Notes on the Manners, Customs, and Conditions of the North American Indians.* 2 vols. 1841. Reprint, New York: Dover, 1973.

————. *O-Kee-Pa: A Religious Ceremony, and Other Customs of the Mandans.* ed. John C. Ewers. New Haven: Yale University Press, 1967.

Crapanzano, Vincent. "Hermes' Dilemma: The Masking of Subversion in Ethnographic Description." In *Writing Culture: The Poetics and Politics of Ethnography; A School of American Research Advanced Seminar*, ed. James Clifford and George E. Marcus, 51–76. Berkeley: University of California Press, 1986.

Dobyns, Henry F. *Their Number Become Thinned: : Native American Population Dynamics in Eastern North America.* Native American Historic Demography Series. Knoxville: University of Tennessee Press and the Newberry Library Center for the History of the American Indian, 1983.

Dorsey, George A. "Ceremonial Organization." In *The Cheyenne*, 57–186. Field Columbian Museum, Anthropological Series 1, vol. 9, no. 1–2. 1905.

Durkheim, Emile. *The Elementary Forms of the Religious Life: A Study in Religious Sociology.* London: George Allen & Unwin, 1915.

Ewers, John C. *The Blackfeet: Raiders on the Northwestern Plains.* Civilization of the American Indian series, vol. 49. Norman: University of Oklahoma Press, 1961.

————. "The Case for Blackfoot Pottery." *American Anthropologist* 47 (1944): 289–99.

————. *The Horse in Blackfoot Indian Culture, With Comparative Material from Other Western Tribes.* Smithsonian Institution, Bureau of American Ethnology Bulletin 159. Washington, D.C., 1955.

————. *Indian Life on the Upper Missouri.* Civilization of the American Indian series, vol. 89. Norman: University of Oklahoma Press, 1968.

————. "The Indian Trade of the Upper Missouri before Lewis and Clark: An Interpretation." *Bulletin of the Missouri Historical Society* 10/4, pt. 1 (1954): 429–46.

———. "Was There a Northwestern Plains Sub-Culture? An Ethnographical Appraisal." *Plains Anthropologist* 12, no. 36 (1967): 167–74.

Fletcher, Alice C. "The Hako: A Pawnee Ceremony." *Twenty-second Annual Report of the Bureau of American Ethnology.* Part 2. 1900–1901.

Geertz, Clifford. *The Interpretation of Cultures: Selected essays.* New York: Basic Books, 1973.

Gill, Sam. *Native American Religions: An Introduction.* The Religious Life of Man Series. Belmont, Calif.: Wadsworth Publishing Co., 1982.

———. *Native American Religious Action: A Performance Approach to Religion.* Studies in Comparative Religion. Columbia: University of South Carolina Press, 1987.

Gilman, Carolyn, and Mary Jane Schneider. *The Way to Independence: Memories of a Hidatsa Indian Family, 1840–1920.* St. Paul: Minnesota Historical Society Press, 1987.

Grinnell, George Bird. *The Cheyenne Indians: Their History and Ways of Life.* 2 vols. Lincoln: University of Nebraska Press, 1972.

———. "Early Cheyenne Villages." *American Anthropologist* 20 (1918): 359–80.

———. "The Great Mysteries of the Cheyenne." *American Anthropologist,* new ser., 16 (1910): 542–75.

———. "Some Early Cheyenne Tales." *Journal of American Folk-Lore* 20 (1907): 169–94.

———. "Some Early Cheyenne Tales II." *Journal of American Folk-Lore* 21 (1908): 269–320.

Hanson, Jeffery R. "Ethnohistorical Problems in the Crow-Hidatsa Separation." *Archaeology in Montana* 20 (1979): 73–86.

———. "Hidatsa Culture Change, 1780–1845: A Cultural Ecological Approach." Ph.D. diss., University of Missouri-Columbia, 1983.

Harrod, Howard L. *The Human Center: Moral Agency in the Social World.* Philadelphia: Fortress Press, 1981.

———. *Mission among the Blackfeet.* Civilization of the American Indian series, vol. 112. Norman: University of Oklahoma Press, 1971.

———. "Missionary Life-World and Native Response: Jesuits in New France." *Sciences Religieuses/Studies in Religion* 13 (1984): 179–82.

———. *Renewing the World: Plains Indian Religion and Morality.* Tucson: University of Arizona Press, 1987.

Hoebel, E. Adamson. *The Cheyennes: Indians of the Great Plains.* 2d ed. Case Studies in Cultural Anthropology. New York: Holt, Rinehart and Winston, 1978.

Holder, Preston. *The Hoe and the Horse on the Plains: A Study of Cultural Development among North American Indians.* Lincoln: University of Nebraska Press, 1970.

Hultkrantz, Ake. *Belief and Worship in Native North America.* Ed. Christopher Vecsey. Ithaca, N.Y.: Syracuse University Press, 1981.

————. *The Religions of the American Indians.* Hermeneutics, Studies in the History of the American Indians. Berkeley: University of California Press, 1979.

————. *Shamanic Healing and Ritual Drama: Health and Medicine in Native North American Religious Traditions.* Health/Medicine and the Faith Traditions series. New York: Crossroad, 1992.

————. *The Study of American Indian Religions.* AAR Studies in Religion, no. 29. New York: Crossroad, 1983.

Hyde, George E. *The Early Blackfeet and Their Neighbors,* Old West Series, no. 2. Denver: John VanMale, 1933.

————. *Life of George Bent Written from His Letters.* Norman: University of Oklahoma Press, 1968.

Irwin, Lee. *The Dream Seekers: Native American Visionary Traditions of the Great Plains.* Civilization of the American Indian series, vol. 213. Norman: University of Oklahoma Press, 1994

Jablow, Joseph. *The Cheyenne in Plains Indian Trade Relations, 1795–1840.* American Ethnological Society Monographs, no. 19. New York: J. J. Augustin, 1951.

Kehoe, Alice B. "The Function of Ceremonial Sexual Intercourse among the Northern Plains Indians." *Plains Anthropologist* 15, no. 47 (1970): 99–103.

Kroeber, Alfred L. "The Ceremonial Organization of the Plains Indians of North America." *Congrès international des Americanistes, XVme session,* 2:53–70. Quebec: Dussault and Prouix, 1907.

Lehmer, Donald J. "The Sedentary Horizon of the Northern Plains." *Southwestern Journal of Anthropology* 10 (1954): 139–59.

Lenski, Gerhard E. *Power and Privilege: A Theory of Social Stratification.* Chapel Hill: University of North Carolina Press, 1984.

Lewis, Oscar. *The Effects of White Contact upon Blackfoot Culture, with Special Reference to the Role of the Fur Trade.* Monographs of the American Ethnological Society, no. 6. Ed. A. Irving Hallowell. New York: J. J. Augustin, 1942.

Lowie, Robert H. *The Crow Indians.* New York: Farrar and Rinehart, 1935.

————. "The Tobacco Society of the Crow Indians." *Anthropological Papers of the American Museum of Natural History* 21 (1920): 103–200.

———. "The Hidatsa Sun Dance." *Anthropological Papers of the American Museum of Natural History* 16 (1921): 411–31.

———. *Indians of the Plains*. Lincoln: University of Nebraska Press, 1982.

———. "Myths and Traditions of the Crow Indians." *Anthropological Papers of the American Museum of Natural History* 25 (1922): 1–308.

———. "Plains Indian Age-Societies: Historical and Comparative Summary." *Anthropological Papers of the American Museum of Natural History* 11 (1916).

———. "The Religion of the Crow Indians." *Anthropological Papers of the American Museum of Natural History* 25 (1922): 309–444.

———. "Some Problems in the Ethnology of the Crow and Village Indians." *American Anthropologist* 14 (1912): 60–71.

———. "Studies in Plains Indian Folklore." *University of California Publications in American Archaeology and Ethnology* 40 (1942–53): 1–28. Berkeley: University of California Press, 1956.

———. "The Sun Dance of the Crow Indians." *Anthropological Papers of the American Museum of Natural History* 16 (1921): 1–50.

———. "The Test Theme in North American Mythology." *Journal of American Folk-Lore* 21 (1908): 97–148.

Mandelbaum, David. "The Plains Cree." *Anthopological Papers of the American Museum of Natural History* 37 (1940–41): 155–316.

Martin, Calvin. *Keepers of the Game: Indian-Animal Relationships and the Fur Trade*. Berkeley: University of California Press, 1978.

Maximilian, Prince of Wied. *Travels in the Interior of North America, 1832–1834*. Early Western Travels, 1748–1846, ed. Reuben Gold Thwaites, vol. 23. Cleveland: Arthur H. Clark Company, 1906.

Medicine Crow, Joseph. *From the Heart of the Crow Country*. Ed. Herman J. Viola. Library of the American Indian. New York: Orion Books, 1992.

Miller, Fred. "The Crow Sun Dance Lodge: Form, Process, and Geometry in the Creation of Sacred Space." *Temenos* 16 (1960): 92–102.

Mishkin, Bernard. *Rank and Warfare among the Plains Indians*. Monographs of the American Ethnological Society 3. New York: J. J. Augustin, 1940.

Moore, John H. *The Cheyenne Nation: A Social and Demographic History*. Lincoln: University of Nebraska Press, 1987.

———. "A Study of Religious Symbolism among the Cheyenne Indians." Ph.D. diss., New York University, 1974.

Morrison, Kenneth M. "Discourse and the Accommodation of Values: Toward a

Revision of Mission History." *Journal of the American Academy of Religion* 53 (1985): 365–82.

Murie, James R. *Ceremonies of the Pawnee*, ed. Douglas R. Parks. 1981. Reprint, Lincoln: University of Nebraska Press with the American Indian Studies Research Institute, 1989.

Oliver, Symmes C. "Ecology and Cultural Continuity as Contributing Factors in the Social Organization of the Plains Indians." *University of California Publications in American Archaeology and Ethnology* 48 (1962): 1–90.

Ottaway, Harold N. "A Possible Origin for the Cheyenne Sacred Arrow Complex." *Plains Anthropologist* 15, no. 47 (1970): 94–98.

Paper, Jordon. *Offering Smoke: The Sacred Pipe and the Native American Religion*. Moscow, Idaho: University of Idaho Press, 1988.

Powell, Peter J. *Sweet Medicine. The Continuing Role of the Sacred Arrows, the Sun Dance, and the Sacred Buffalo Hat in Northern Cheyenne History*. 2 vols. Norman: University of Oklahoma Press, 1969.

Randolph, Richard W. *Sweet Medicine.*. Caldwell, Idaho: Caxton Printers, 1937.

Sapir, Edward. *Time Perspective in Aboriginal American Culture*. Geological Survey of Canada 13, Anthropological Series. Ottawa, 1916.

Schlesier, Karl. "Rethinking the Midewiwin and the Plains Ceremonial Called the Sun Dance." *Plains Anthropologist* 35, no. 127 (1990): 1–27.

———. *The Wolves of Heaven: Cheyenne Shamanism, Ceremonies, and Prehistoric Origins*. Civilization of the American Indian series, vol. 183. Norman: University of Oklahoma Press, 1987.

Secoy, Frank Raymond. *Changing Military Patterns on the Great Plains*. Monographs of the American Ethnological Society 21. New York: J. J. Augustin, 1953.

Simms, S. C. "Cultivation of 'Medicine Tobacco' by the Crows: A Preliminary Paper." *American Anthropologist* 6 (1904): 331–35.

———. *Traditions of the Crows*. Publications of the Field Museum of Natural History, Anthropological Series, vol. 2, no. 6. Chicago, 1903.

Spier, Leslie. "The Sun Dance of the Plains Indians: Its Development and Diffusion." *Anthropological Papers of the American Museum of Natural History* 16 (1921): 451–527.

Stewart, Frank H. *Fundamentals of Age-Group Systems*. New York: Academic Press, 1977.

Teit, James. "The Salishan Tribes of the Western Plateaus." Ed. Franz Boas. *Forty-Fifth Annual Report of the Bureau of American Ethnology*, 45 (1927–28): 23–396.

Voget, Fred W. *The Shoshoni-Crow Sun Dance.* Norman: University of Oklahoma
Press, 1984.

Weber, Max. *The Sociology of Religion.* Trans. Ephraim Fischoff. Boston: Beacon
Press, 1963.

Whorf, Benjamin Lee. *Language, Thought, and Reality: Selected Writings of Benjamin
Lee Whorf.* Cambridge: Technology Press of the Massachusetts Institute of
Technology, 1956.

Wildschut, William. *Crow Indian Medicine Bundles.* Contributions from the Museum of the American Indian, Heye Foundation 17. Ed. John Ewers. New
York, 1960.

Will, George F., and George E. Hyde. *Corn among the Indians of the Upper Missouri.*
Lincoln: University of Nebraska Press, 1917.

Wilson, Gilbert L. "Hidatsa-Mandan Report, Fort Berthold Reservation." Vols. 7,
10, and 16. 1908–14. Typescript in the Minnesota Historical Society.

Wissler, Clark. "Ceremonial Bundles of the Blackfoot Indians." *Anthropological Papers of the American Museum of Natural History* 7 (1912): 69–289.

———. "Comparative Study of Pawnee and Blackfoot Rituals." *Proceedings of the
Nineteenth International Congress of Americanists.* 1915. Reprint, Nendeln,
Liechtenstein: Kraus Reprint, 1968.

———. "The Diffusion of Culture in the Plains of North America." *Congrès international des Americanistes,* XVme session. 2 : 39–63. Quebec: Dussault and
Prouix, 1907.

———. "The Influence of the Horse in the Development of Plains Culture." *American Anthropologist* 16 (1914): 1–25.

Wissler, Clark, and D. C. Duvall. "Blackfoot Mythology." *Anthropological Papers of
the American Museum of Natural History* 2 (1908): 1–163.

Wood, W. Raymond. *Biesterfeldt: A Post-Contact Coalescent Site on the Northeastern
Plains.* Smithsonian Contributions to Anthropology No. 15. Washingon,
D.C.: Smithsonian Institution Press, 1971.

———. *An Interpretation of Mandan Culture History.* Smithsonian Institution, Bureau of American Ethnology Bulletin 198. Washington, D.C., 1967.

———. *The Origins of the Hidatsa Indians: A Review of Ethnohistorical and Traditional
Data.* Reprints in Anthropology, vol. 32. Lincoln: J & L Reprint Co.,
1986.

———. "Plains Trade in Prehistoric and Protohistoric Intertribal Relations." In
Anthropology on the Great Plains, ed. W. Raymond Wood and Margot Liberty, 98–109. Lincoln: University of Nebraska Press, 1980.

————, ed. "Trends in Middle Missouri Prehistory: A Festschrift Honoring the Contributions of Donald J. Lehmer." Memoir 13. *Plains Anthropologist* 22, no. 78, pt. 2 (1977): 1–185.

Wood, W. Raymond, and Alan S. Downer. "Notes on the Crow-Hidatsa Schism." *Plains Anthropologist* 22, no. 78, pt. 2, Memoir 13 (1977): 83–100.

Wood, W. Raymond, and Margot Liberty. *Anthropology on the Great Plains*. Lincoln: University of Nebraska Press, 1980.

INDEX

Adoption rituals, 85

Age graded societies, 6, 8, 9, 58, 67, 68, 111 n. 8
    among the Blackfeet, 11
    and transfer of power, 118 n. 11

Alberta, ix

Algonquian, 8, 9, 12, 13, 113 n. 43
    sexual transfer of power among, 9

Amahamis, 9, 113 n. 38

American Fur Company, 10

Anderson, Karen, 131 n. 5

Animal rituals, 69–77

Aortas (Cheyenne division), 93, 130 n. 41

Apaches, 14

Arapahoes, 6, 7, 8, 12, 13
    and Atsinas, 5
    migration of, 14, 15

Arikaras, 7, 65, 92

Arrow Man, in the Awatixa traditions, 39, 89

Assiniboines, 5, 6, 12, 69, 88

Astral beings, 105–6
    in Crow traditions, 84–87

Atsinas, 5, 6, 7, 8, 14, 111 n. 8
    and Crees, 12
    membership purchase in men's migration of, 12–14
    societies, 9

Awatixas (Hidatsa division), 37, 63, 64, 71
    and Cheyennes, 89, 92
    origin tradition of, 38–40

Awatixa Village, 54, 56

Awaxawis (Hidatsa division), 37, 63, 64, 69
    and Cheyennes, 93
    origin tradition of, 38

Awigaxas (Mandan division), 34

Bear Butte (Nowahwas), 91, 95

Bears Arm, 94

Bellah, Robert, 131 n. 1
Berdache (third gender)
    becoming a berdache, 117 n. 29
    in Northern Plains societies, 22
    role in Crow Sun Dance, 120 n. 29
    role in ritual preparation, 59
    role in social change, 68
    social status of, 68
Black Eagle, 118 n. 4
Blackfeet
    Algonquian speaking, 5
    and Atsinas, 5, 13
    and Cheyennes, 13
    divisions of, 110 n. 4
    and fur trade, 10–11
    and Mandans and Hidatsas, 10–11
    migration of, 13–14
    and Pawnees, 7, 8
    and sexual transfer of power, 9–10
    worldview, 109 n. 2
Black Hills, South Dakota, 13, 15, 67,
    88, 89, 91, 95
Black Medicine, in Mandan origin
    traditions, 41
Black Mouths (Hidatsa and Mandan), 64
Blood Clot Man
    in the Blackfeet tradition, 123 n. 38
    in Hidatsa Buffalo Corral ritual,
        123 n. 38
    in Hidatsa Imitating Buffalo rit-
        ual, 70
Bloods (Blackfeet division), 11
    Horn Society of, 9
Boas, Franz, 110 n. 5
Boller, Henry, 118 n. 14
Boundary Mound burial site, 31
Bowers, Alfred W., 63, 66, 67, 116 n.

12, 119 n. 15, 122 nn. 24, 31,
    123 n. 39
Bruner, Edward M., 8, 121 n. 5
Buffalo
    and connection with humans, 76
    dependence upon, among Plains so-
        cieties, 4
    in Hidatsa Naxpike ritual, 57
    in Hidatsa origin traditions, 39
    importance to ritual, 48, 70–73
    in Mandan Okipa ritual, 46
    ritual renewal of, 48, 50–51, 69, 70
    ritual significance of, 31–32
Buffalo Bird Woman, 38, 116 n. 21
Buffalo rituals and ceremonies
    Buffalo Corral, 123 nn. 36, 38
    Buffalo Dance, 69
    Buffalo Neckbone, 123 n. 36
    Imitating Buffalo, 70
    Painted Red Stick, 71–73, 76,
        123 n. 41
    White Buffalo Cow society ritual,
        75–76
Buffalo Woman
    in Hidatsa Imitating Buffalo ritual, 70
    in Painted Red Stick ritual, 72
Bullchild, Percy, 109 n. 2
Bull That Goes Hunting, 126 n. 6

Canada, ix, 12, 13
Cannonball River, 33, 41
Catlin, George, 117 n. 1, 118 nn. 12,
    14, 120 n. 33
Center Pole, 57, 59
Charred Body
    in origin tradition of Awatixas, 39,
        89, 90, 93, 94, 95

origin traditions, 53, 57, 92, 125 n. 5, 128 n. 24, 130 n. 41
    summary of, 89–90
Cheyennes, 5, 6, 82, 110 n. 6
    contact with Awaxawis, 93–94
    contact with Hidatsas, 92–96
    development of social identity, 93, 130 n. 44
    divisions among, 131 n. 45
    formation of new social identity, 94, 97
    history of, 87–89
    and Mandans, 92
    migrations of, 12–13, 15, 30, 88, 127 n. 16
    missionary contact with, 129 n. 28
    and sexual transfer of power, 8
    transformation of religious traditions and practices, 89–97
Coeur d'Alenes, and influence of the horse upon, 15–16
Comanches, 6, 14
Corn Father, in Mandan origin traditions, 37
Corn Priests (Mandan), 53
Corn Silk, in Mandan Red Stick Ritual, 71
Coyote (First Man), in Mandan origin traditions, 36
Crees, 5, 88, 12
Crow Bull, 94
Crows, xix, 6, 30, 82, 117 n. 27, 128 n. 25
    migration of, 12, 15
    origin traditions of, 83–84
    separation from the Hidatsas, 5, 33, 82, 83, 86, 125 n. 4

and transformation of religious traditions and practices, 82–87
Cultural interchange, between village and hunter societies, 8–9

Dakotas, 15
Downer, Alan S., 125 n. 4
Dreams and visions, in Plains societies, 21, 26–27, 28, 84
Durkheim, Emile, 131 n. 1

Eaters (Cheyenne division), 93, 130 n. 41
Erect Horns, in Sutaio traditions, 88
Ewers, John C., 34–35, 110 n. 4, 118 n. 14

Female Earth (Creator), in Hidatsa origin traditions, 38
Female figures
    Charred Body's Sister, in Awatixa origin tradition, 39, 89
    in Hidatsa and Mandan origin traditions, 40
    Holy Women, 41
    Holy Women of the groves of the four directions, 41
    Old Woman Who Never Dies (goddess of all vegetation), 41, 43, 77, 78, 79, 94, 129 n. 28
    in symbolism of Hidatsa and Mandan societies, 41
    Village Old Woman, 40–41, 70, 117 n. 29
    Woman Above, 41
First Creator (Coyote), of Hidatsa proper and Awatixa origin traditions, 38, 70, 94

First Man (Coyote) of Mandan origin
    traditions, 36
First Worker (Creator), of Hidatsa ori-
    gin traditions, 38
Flatheads, 6
Fort Atkinson, 118 n. 14
Fort Clark, 45
Fort Yates, 92, 93, 130 n. 41
Friendly relations theory of culture
    change (Wissler), 6–7

Gender
    influence on participation in soci-
        eties, 75–77
    influence on structure of ritual pro-
        cesses, 76–77
    and ownership of sacred bundles, 77
Gender relations
    in Cheyenne traditions, 129 n. 29
    effect of warfare on, 64
    in Mandan and Hidatsa origin
        traditions, 21–22
    primordial order of, 22
Gender roles
    in Mandan Okipa ritual, 49–51
    reversals of, 49–50, 117 n. 27
Good Bear, 41
Good Furred Robe
    in Mandan origin traditions, 36–
        37, 47, 78
    tradition (Mandan), 22, 123 n. 42
Grand River, 117 n. 2
Gulf of Mexico, 36

Heart River, 22, 33, 34, 36, 116 n. 12,
    38, 42, 64
Hidatsas, x, 30
    age graded societies, 7

and Crows, 5
and culture change, 6–12, 62ff.,
    113 n. 38
female figures in origin traditions,
    40–41
female symbolism in society, 41–
    43, 45
origin traditions, 33–34,
relation to environment, 21–22
religion and culture of, xviii
settlement along Missouri River,
    31–33
and sexual transfer of power, 9
and smallpox epidemics, 63
social organization of, 55
Hoita in Mandan Okipa ritual, 46, 69
Holder, Preston, 8
Horses, impact of, on Plains societies,
    14–16
Hultkrantz, Ake, 132 n. 7
Hyde, George, 12–14, 113 nn. 38, 43

Indian: use of term by author, 109 n. 3
Indian Christianity, 106–7
Intermarriage, as source of social
    change, 64, 65
Iowa, ix

Kehoe, Alice B., 8–10, 112 n. 20
Kiowas, 6, 15
Knife River, 22, 33, 38, 117 n. 2
Kroeber, A. L., 111 n. 9
Kurz, Rudolph Frederick, 120 n. 33

Lake Superior, 13, 88
Lake Winnipeg, 12
Leech Lake, Minnesota, 127 n. 16
Lehmer, Donald J., 8

Lenski, Gerhard E., 110 n. 2

Lewis, Oscar, 10–11

Lewis and Clark, 88, 123 n. 39

Like-a-Fishhook Village, 56, 118 n. 14

Lodge Boy in Hidatsa Charred Body traditions, 39–40, 89

Lone Man
in Hidatsa traditions, 70
in Mandan Okipa ritual, 46–49, 52
in Mandan traditions, 35–36, 38

Long Arm, in Hidatsa Charred Body traditions, 40–41, 54, 56, 58–59, 90

Lowie, Robert, 65, 66, 126 nn. 6, 8, 127 n. 12

Mandans, x, 4, 30, 45
age graded societies, 7
and culture change, 6–12, 62 ff., 113 n. 38
divisions of, 34
female figures in origin traditions, 40–41
female symbolism in society, 41–43, 45
origin traditions, 33–37
relation to environment, 21–22
religion and culture of, xviii
settlement along Missouri River, 31–33
and sexual transfer of power, 9
and smallpox epidemics, 34, 62, 64
social organization of, 64

Mandelbaum, David, 12

Man With No Head, in Hidatsa Charred Body traditions, 39, 89

Marcus, George E., 117 n. 1

Martin, Calvin, 113 n. 35

Matthews, Washington, 118 n. 14

Maximilian, Alexander Philipp, 34, 123 n. 39

Maynadier, Lieutenant Henry E., 118 n. 14

Medicine Crow, 83, 84

Medicine Crow, Joseph, 109 n. 1, 126 n. 8

Men's societies, development of, 15

Menstruation
and symbolic contamination, 76
and symbolic fertility, 80

Migration narratives and origin traditions, 22–23

Migrations, as source of culture change among Plains societies, 12–14

Minnesota, ix, 93

Mishkin, Bernard, 15

Mississippi River, 36, 88

Missouri River, 14, 15, 21, 22, 34–38, 45, 52, 62, 64, 71, 78, 89, 92, 93, 96, 117 n. 2, 130 n. 41

Missouri River region, early settlement of, 31–33

Montana, ix

Moon in Painted Red Stick ritual, 72

Moore, John H., 127 n. 16, 129 nn. 26, 35, 36, 130 nn. 41, 44

Morgan, Lewis Henry, 119 n. 14

Mountain Crows, 33

Museum of the Plains Indian (Browning, Mont.), 109 n. 1

Native American: use of term by author, 109 n. 3

Naxpike, or Hidebeating ceremony (Hidatsa), 43, 45, 53–59, 63, 65, 77, 90, 93, 94, 122 n. 17, 125 n. 5

Naxpike bundle, 43, 54

Nebraska, ix

North Dakota, ix, 32, 33, 39, 93

Northern Plains, ix, 5, 6, 14, 23, 54, 57, 58, 62, 81, 97, 109 n. 3, 125 n. 1

Northern Plains religions
  and animals, 35, 41, 48
  as both conservative and innovative, 96
  and contemporary Indian peoples, 106–7
  creator figures in, 20–21
  and cultural boundaries, 25–26, 33–43, 65, 100
  culture heroes in, 22–23
  and death, 21–22, 104
  and effectiveness, 103
  and European Christianity, 103–6
  historical context of, 102–3
  hunting symbolism in, 57
  and monotheism, 104–5
  and natural environment, 47, 79
  role in legitimating social change, 66–80
  sense of difference in, 100
  and sense of place, 22
  sharing religious meaning, 103
  as source of culture change, 14, 17, 27–30, 125 n. 1
  as source of social identity and continuity, 20–27, 43, 45, 52, 53, 59, 83, 87, 96–97
  as source of social status, 46, 59
  sources for interpretation, xv–xvii
  and state-based societies, 100
  as structure for Native American social worlds, 99–100

and the supernatural, 105
  transcendent dimensions of, 59, 105–6
  and transformation of religious ritual and practice, 82–87, 89–97

Northern Plains societies
  contact with European culture, 27–28, 74
  encounter with fur trade, 10–12
  major divisions of, 3–4
  matrilineal organization and influence among, 9, 49, 53
  migrations of, 12–14
  and the preservation of social identity, 102
  symbolic universe of, 38–43

Nuitadis (Mandan division), 34

Nuptadis (Mandan division), 34

Ojibways, 6

Okipa ceremony (Mandan), 9, 25, 43, 63, 65, 69, 123 n. 17

Old Man Coyote (First Worker), in Crow origin traditions, 83

Old Woman Crawling, 94

Old Woman Who Never Dies tradition, 41–43

Oral traditions
  importance of, xvii, 99–100
  precarious nature of, 101
  and sense of cultural continuity, 69, 80

Origin traditions, 20–23
  gender relations in, 21–22
  geography in, 22
  missionary influence on, 38, 116 n. 12

Pawnees, 7, 27

Pemmican, Porcupine, 120 n. 27

Plains Crees, 6

Plains Indians, 54, 121 n. 2

Plant life (agriculture)

and religion, 35, 41, 77–80

ritual renewal of, 48, 49

Plenty Hawk, 84

Powder River, 67

Raven Necklace, in Hidatsa buffalo

calling ritual, 69

Red River, 13, 14

Reorganization, of Hidatsa and Man-

dan societies, 64–80

Ritual adoption, 66–67

Ritual and ceremony

body painting in, 47–48, 49, 51,

53, 58, 86, 118 n. 14

and everyday world, 58

Grass Dance, 67–68, 122 nn. 24, 29

Hako ritual (Pawnee), 7

Horn Society ritual (Blood), 10

Matoki (Blood), 11

Midewiwin, 121 n. 2

Pawnee Hako ritual, 7, 111 n. 12

Peace Pipe or Calumet cere-

mony, 7

Snow Owl (Mandan), 124 n. 47

See also Naxpike; Okipa ceremony;

Sun Dance

Ritual knowledge

transfer of, 46, 55, 58

and transfer of power, 50

Ritual offerings, 84

Ritual suffering, 63, 118 n. 14

in Hidatsa Naxpike, 58

in Mandan Okipa, 51–52

as religious action, 52

River Crows, 33

Robe bundle (Mandan), 77

Sacred Arrows

Cheyenne, 25, 91, 95, 96, 129 n. 29

Hidatsa, 56, 57, 92

Sacred bundles

and "bundle complex," 11,

112 n. 31

combination of materiality and po-

tency in, 120 n. 25

role in rituals, 45

and social transformation, 29–30

as source of cultural continuity, 23–

28, 65, 102

Salish, 15

Santee Sioux, 67

Sapir, Edward, 113 n. 43

Sarsis, 5, 6

Saskatchewan, ix

Scattercorn, 48

Schlesier, Karl, 130 n. 44

Secoy, Frank, 14–15

Seen-from-Afar, 11

Sexual behavior within ritual

contexts, 50, 78–79,

cultural significance of, 50–51

mimetic sexual rituals, 49

in Painted Red Stick ritual, 72–74

Sexual transfers of power

among Algonquians, 9

among Blackfeet, 9–10

among Hidatsas, 9

among Mandans, 124 n. 47

among Plains societies, 8–10

Sheyenne River, 92, 95
Shoshoneans (northern), 14
Shuswaps, 15
Simms, S. C., 126n. 6
Sioux, 64, 88
Smallpox epidemics
    of 1781–82, 93, 121nn. 2, 5
    of 1837, 62–64, 121n. 2
    and Plains societies, 16
South Dakota, ix, 32
Spier, Leslie, 120n. 22
Spring Boy, of Hidatsa Charred body
    traditions, 40–41, 58–59, 89
Stewart, Frank H., 111n. 8
Strikes Both Ways, 84
Sun
    in Crow origin traditions, 83
    in Hidatsa origin traditions, 41
    in Painted Red Stick ritual, 72
Sun Dance, 5, 15, 25, 26, 40, 54, 57,
    86, 87, 88, 110n. 6, 125n. 5,
    130n. 44
    origin of, 110n. 6, 121n. 2
    use of pipes in, 67
    variations of, 120n. 22, 127n. 19,
    128n. 24
Sutaios, 88, 93, 129n. 36
    and origin of Cheyenne Sun Dance,
    110n. 6
Sweat Lodge, 58, 86
Sweet Medicine
    Cheyenne, 90–92, 95, 96, 97,
    129nn. 29, 31, 36
    Mandan, 42
    tradition (Cheyenne), 93, 95, 128
    n. 24, 129n. 35, 130nn. 41, 44

Thompsons, 15
Tiet, James, 16
Tobacco
    as central to religious practice, 21
    in Crow society, 83, 126n. 8
    as culture hero in Crow traditions
    (Star Man), 87, 97
    in Mandan origin tradition, 35
    ritual, 83
Tobacco Society, 127n. 15
    divisions and structure of, 84
    initiation process, 85–86
    and the planting of tobacco, 86
    role in maintaining and renewing
    symbolic boundaries, 87
Transfer of power in Plains culture
    through exchange of property, 26
    from father to son (Hidatsa), 40, 70
    through kinship, 26, 53
    through sexual intercourse, 72–73
Trickster figures, 118n. 14
    description of, 20, 49
    role in Plains religions, 20
Two Men (Lodge Boy and Spring Boy),
    in Hidatsa Charred Body tradition,
    40, 54, 77, 89, 90, 94

Unknown Man (Hidatsa), 40, 54, 55,
    77, 90, 93

Visions and dreams
    and legitimation of social change, 66
    in Naxpike ritual, 56
    in Okipa ritual, 46

Walking Chief, 73
Walking Soldier, 68

Washburn, North Dakota, 39

White Calf, 35, 47, 118n. 7

Wife surrender practices, 8–9,
118n. 11

Wilson, Gilbert L., 116nn. 20, 21

Wissler, Clark, 5–7, 15, 110nn. 5, 6

Wolf Chief, 36, 39, 67, 73, 74,
122n. 24

Women
link to fertility rituals, 76–80
participation in membership rites,
86, 118n. 11
particpation in ritual, 49–50, 55,
57, 58, 73, 76–80, 119n. 14,
127n. 12

participation in Tobacco society, 84
and power in Mandan and Hidatsa
societies, 124n. 56
roles in ritual, 11
sexual exploitation of, 73–74
as symbolic source of fecundity, 49

Women's societies
Goose Society, 79, 80, 124n. 51
Holy Women's Society (Hidatsa), 57
White Buffalo Cow society, 74–
77, 80

Wood, W. Raymond, 116n. 20, 125n. 4

Wyoming, ix

ABOUT THE AUTHOR

Howard L. Harrod became interested in Native Americans during his child-hood in Oklahoma. After earning his doctorate at Yale University, he taught in the areas of the sociology of religion, religion and culture, and Native American religions. He presently teaches at Vanderbilt University, where he is Oberlin Alumni Professor of Social Ethics and Sociology of Religion and Professor of Religious Studies. In 1971 he published *Mission among the Blackfeet* (reissued in 1999), which focused on the impact of the missionary movement, both Protes-tant and Catholic, on Native American culture and religion. In 1981 he pub-lished *The Human Center: Moral Agency in the Social World,* a critical rethinking of themes in the sociology of religion. The application of this theoretical perspec-tive resulted in the publication of *Renewing the World: Plains Indian Religion and Morality* with the University of Arizona Press in 1987. *Becoming and Remaining a People* extends this perspective and deals with the importance of religion for understanding social change as well as social continuity within Native Ameri-can societies. His latest book, *The Animals Came Dancing: Native American Sacred Ecology and Animal Kinship,* was published by the University of Arizona Press in 2000.